A Forgotten Wilderness

Nature's Hidden Relationships in West Central Idaho

Matthew Deren

THE
DONNING COMPANY
PUBLISHERS

The Donning Company Publishers
184 Business Park Drive, Suite 206
Virginia Beach, VA 23462

Steve Mull, General Manager
Barbara Buchanan, Office Manager
Pamela Koch, Senior Editor
Chad Harper Casey, Graphic Designer
Priscilla Odango, Imaging Artist
Katie Gardner, Project Research Coordinator
Tonya Hannink, Marketing Specialist
Pamela Engelhard, Marketing Advisor

Cathleen Norman, Project Director

Library of Congress Cataloging-in-Publication Data

Deren, Matthew.
 A forgotten wilderness : nature's hidden relationships in west central Idaho / Matthew Deren.
   p. cm.
 Includes index.
 ISBN 978-1-57864-658-6 (soft cover : alk. paper)
 1. Natural history—Idaho—Pictorial works. 2. Wilderness areas—Idaho—Pictorial works. 3.
Landscapes—Idaho—Pictorial works. 4. Seasons—Idaho—Pictorial works. 5. Idaho—Pictorial works.
6. Natural history—Idaho. 7. Wilderness areas—Idaho. 8. Idaho—Description and travel. 9. Idaho—
Geography. 10. Idaho—Environmental conditions. I. Title.
 QH105.I2D37 2010
 508.796—dc22

                                        2010042279

Printed in the United States of America at Walsworth Publishing Company

Contents

This book, *A Forgotten Wilderness*, is not just a collection of beautiful pictures of the flora, fauna, and birdlife of West Central Idaho. It is an outstanding educational presentation of how and why we are so fortunate to be home where the Pacific Climate Pattern meets the Continental Climate Pattern.

The transition zone between the two is in a steep canyon north of McCall, Idaho. Majestic towering peaks of granite and deep canyons make much of this pristine area inaccessible to vehicular traffic, thereby protecting this geologic time zone from development and intrusion of activities that would adversely affect the area. There are no sharp boundaries but unique areas still remaining as God created them.

To slowly move through this fascinating book is a travel through time, giving us a glimpse of those special places and their inhabitants that are constantly moving and changing in geologic time, glacial as it is, which is determined by climate change. We current residents of Central Idaho are fortunate to enjoy what has been given to us and depicted in this book, even if we have never stopped to think why it is there at our doorstep with all its beauty.

The abundance of wildlife, birds, plant life, and towering conifers sets this area apart from the deserts of the South and the rainforests of the Northwest, each of which influences the imaginary boundaries of unofficial wild areas as *A Forgotten Wilderness*. The diversity of animal life as it has changed over millions of years is documented not only by history but also by the photos you will enjoy on your journey through this book.

With his flawless photography and historic commentary, Matthew Deren and Brundage Mountain have given us an accurate and beautiful history lesson on how our priceless area has come to be.

Cecil D. Andrus

The Honorable Cecil D. Andrus "Cece" is Idaho's only four-term governor. His four years as U.S. Secretary of the Interior also made him the first Idahoan to serve in a presidential cabinet. Cece has earned a national reputation for being able to strike a wise balance between often conflicting conservation and development positions. During his years in public service, Cece championed improvements in Idaho's educational system, presided over periods of sustained economic growth, helped create Alaska's great national parks, and pushed a national strategy for safe disposal of nuclear waste. Cece founded and now directs the Andrus Center for Public Policy at Boise State University. Since 1995, the Andrus Center has organized major conferences on Western public lands issues, national fire policy, endangered species issues, and the economy of the rural West.

An intimate look at a forgotten wilderness

The natural story of West Central Idaho, the hidden transition zone of the Rockies

The title, *A Forgotten Wilderness*, refers much more to those forgotten forces and connections that drive life on earth than it does to any place or region in particular. These relationships, once the accepted force of everyday life, have diminished in importance in our minds and culture. This web of interconnection still, however unnoticed, drives completely the living world, including our connection to and place within.

This book is really only a small part of a very large story—a window to a few hidden scenes from a quiet place on the Pacific Slope of the Rockies, a small region where a fascinating shift in the natural landscape of North America takes hold. It is in this transitional land where large changes begin: the Continental meets the Maritime, the South transforms to the North, the Dry becomes Wet, and the Cultivated meets the Wild. This place has no name and no exact boundaries, though it currently occurs in a section of the Northern Rockies roughly coinciding with West Central Idaho. This continental transition point has not always been situated where it is today. Within the span of geologic time, this transition area has been in constant motion, drifting north, south, east, and west in cyclical response to the ever-changing climate that comprised the last two million years and beyond.

As all explorations must start somewhere, the present is an obvious place to begin. Though we focus on this one unique area, the interconnections and patterns within this book underlie the whole of North America and, to a larger extent, the entirety of the natural world.

In the end, "the forgotten wilderness" is nothing more than the forgotten view of the world as a place of infinite interconnection, and thus can be rediscovered anywhere, not just in the places we call "wilderness."

All photographs were taken by the author on location of wild, free-roaming, unhabituated animals. Strategically placed motion-activated cameras, as well as a Pentax k10d digital SLR often mounted on an 80mm Kowa scope, account for all images. All drawings and maps were custom-built for this geographical area by the author.

Opposite page: Mother lion rests in a patch of pipsissewa in a stand of dense Douglas fir. On a ridge far above Hazard Creek in early summer, her adolescent cub, its spots nearly faded, plays nearby.

Wolves have become a symbol of
controversy in the West, but the fight is
more about our future than their own.

8

Geology, Geography, Climate

Ecoregions of the Rockies

Coastal Forests

Northern Rockies

West Central
Transition Zone

Pacific

Central Rockies

Continental

Southern Rockies

West Central Idaho: The Big Picture

Our section of the Rockies is a difficult area to define. The Rockies can be separated into two fairly different regions: a Pacific-influenced (northern) complex and a Continental-influenced (central/southern) complex. The simplified trend is this: the Pacific climate brings inland moist winters and drier summers. The Continental influence brings colder, drier winters and wetter summers. The difficulty in labeling our area of West Central Idaho is that we fit into neither and both at the same time. We are in the transition area between a more Pacific type of Rockies and a more Continental type—a mixed zone. Though difficult to label, our area benefits from a complexity and variety of species not found in either region.

There are no true lines or boundaries. Spring, summer, fall, and winter converge. The change from season to season does not occur like a page turning on the calendar; instead, it flips back and forth forming a blurry line. If we look closely, we can always see signs of the previous seasons and the future ones to come—pockets still covered in snow, plants gone to seed, flowers in bud, energy returning to the roots—all four seasons in a single day.

The Concept of "Variety of the Edge"

Picture a large meadow surrounded by dense forest in every direction. On average, wildlife and plant variety will peak at the edge between the two habitats. The deep forest has good cover for hiding, but little light reaches the ground. Here we have only shade-tolerant plants beneath the trees. In the meadow center, we have nourishing grasses in full sun, but nowhere to hide and no room for plants to break through the established turf. At the edge, we have everything: layered shade and sun, good browse and good cover, and a maximum variety of plants. Plant and cover opportunities attract the great variety of wildlife of the hybrid zones.

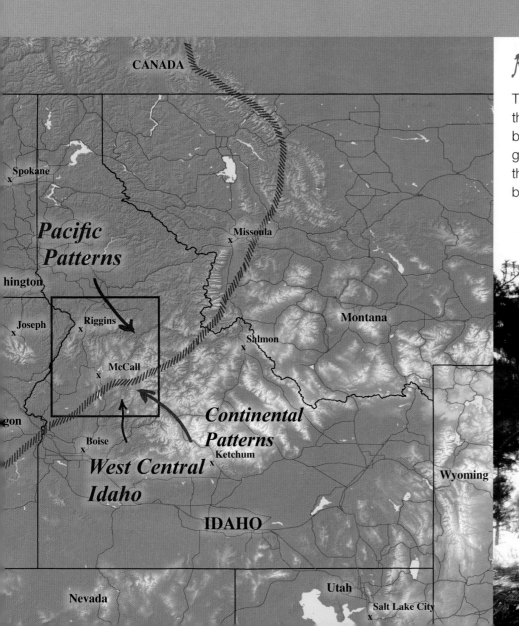

CANADA

Spokane
x

Pacific Patterns

hington

Missoula
x

Joseph
x

Riggins
x

Montana

Salmon
x

McCall
x

Continental Patterns

gon

Boise
x

Ketchum
x

West Central Idaho

Wyoming

IDAHO

Nevada

Utah

Salt Lake City
x

Regional View: West Central Idaho

The purple line on the map represents an average boundary line between the Maritime and Continental influences over the Inland Northwest. The line blurs and moves with time, but it is most apparent, or rather changes with the greatest force, in the region around McCall. It is here in these mountain ranges that the first major inland barrier of eastward Pacific air occurs. In a sense, this barrier forces a resolution between the two major climate regimes.

Closer View: West Central Idaho

A year-round balance of weather provides for some of the most engaging outdoor recreation in North America. It is a nearly perfect place to explore the full depth of natural relationships.

Granite Batholiths

The Needles (left) are one of many examples of the now-exposed granite batholith that underlies most of Central Idaho. The batholith, meaning "deep stone," refers to its formation—granite cooling at depth. The later uplift of the Rockies and the subsequent erosive forces raised and exposed the massive granite domes.

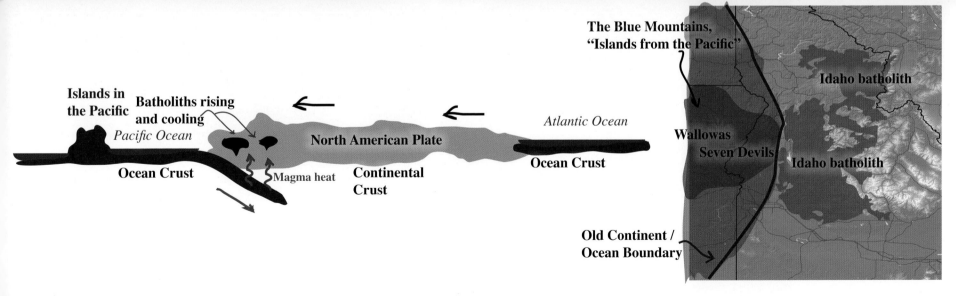

Islands in the Pacific

Batholiths rising and cooling

Pacific Ocean

Ocean Crust

North American Plate

Magma heat

Continental Crust

Atlantic Ocean

Ocean Crust

The Blue Mountains, "Islands from the Pacific"

Idaho batholith

Wallowas

Seven Devils

Idaho batholith

Old Continent / Ocean Boundary

Former location of the Pacific ocean

Former Continent Boundary

Oregon

Riggins

Main Salmon

Little Salmon

McCall

Idaho

Where tectonic plates collide and ocean crust is pulled beneath a continental land mass, volcanic activity, mountain building, and hot springs result.

Inset, next page: Requiring higher pH environments, the helleborine orchid blooms are limited to a handful of select hot springs. This one was found along the South Fork of the Salmon River in early July.

When plates collide, mountains, hot springs, and volcanoes result.

Old World and New World Become One

The idea of an Old and a New World is a matter of timing; the land bridge connecting Siberia and Alaska appeared at every major glaciation in the last two million years. Each time that a significant portion of the Earth's water became locked in the growing polar caps, sea levels dropped hundreds of feet, revealing the shallow Bering Sea shelf—the land connection between the continents.

Viewed in geologic time, the land bridge appeared and disappeared like a high and low tide. Crossing the shelf far back in the glacial cycles were creatures such as the moose, the brown bear, the gray wolf, and the flying squirrel. We think of these now as very North American wildlife, but there was a time when they were not.

The crossing that without question had the greatest impact on the wildlife of the Americas was the most recent land bridge event (13,500 years ago) when, for the first time, humans arrived.

There are New World animals, such as the mountain lion and the pronghorn antelope, and there are animals that came from the Old World, such as the gray wolf and the brown bear. Our mountain lions evolved here, and they have always lived exclusively in the New World. By contrast, the moose is from the Old World, having crossed the Bering Land Bridge like so many others that we now consider to be "native wildlife."

Siberia

Beringia

Receding Ice Sheets

Migration Pathways

The Continental Ice Sheet

Alpine Glaciation

Alpine Glaciation

At the peak of each ice age, forests overtook our steppes, and plants and animals of the Great Basin retreated south and west. We have been in a stage of glacial retreat for a dozen millennia, and slowly these plants and animals have been returning north, part of a cycle that has been occurring for the past two million years.

Alpine Glaciers

Alpine glaciation refers to the islands of year-round ice confined to the highest elevations.

The town of McCall is situated at the melting point of one such glacier, as a river of ice dug and then deposited rock and soil at the south end of what is now Payette Lake, scouring a depression for a deep lake and forming the dam at the glacier's terminus.

Looking at Payette Lake today, it is interesting to picture it at the time of its creation—scoured rock, free of soil and plants, with a fresh deep lake churning against barren shores.

Inset map: Debris from many glacial episodes slowly filled the Long and Meadows Valley with eroded soil, forming lakes of sediment.

Fault Block Valley

Early in Formation

Block

Jughandle

New Valley Floor

Sediment Fill

Block

Long Valley is essentially a giant flat lake of sediment—a wide valley created not by a river but by the faulting of the earth. It is a fault block that dropped and then, through the erosive force of glaciers, slowly filled with crushed rock and soil, forming what is now a "lake" of earth thousands of feet thick.

Background image, full page: River Ranch, McCall; Long Valley looking south

Inset, above left: The most recent glacier to push into the valley left evidence of its passing in the giant boulders not yet buried.

Lick Creek Summit: The Classic U-shaped Glacial Valley

Not one river of ice, but dozens over millions of years carved our glacial high-elevation valleys. Areas of bare rock and twisted trees growing from cracks bring images of the recent retreat of ice and the cyclical recolonization of plants.

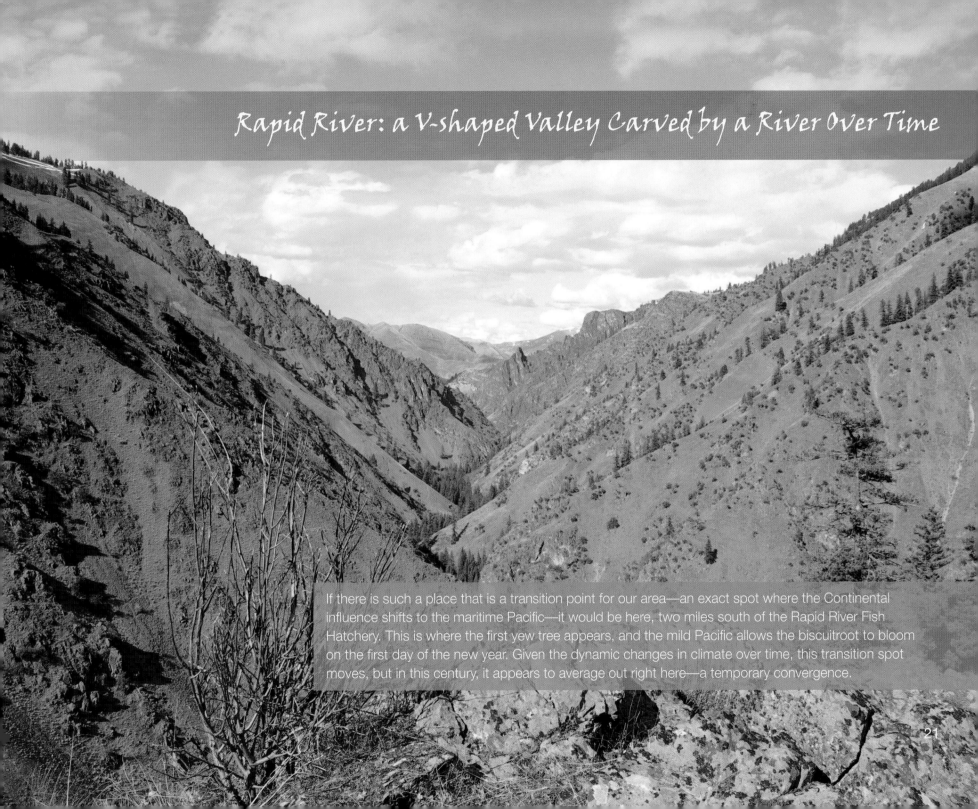

Rapid River: a V-shaped Valley Carved by a River Over Time

If there is such a place that is a transition point for our area—an exact spot where the Continental influence shifts to the maritime Pacific—it would be here, two miles south of the Rapid River Fish Hatchery. This is where the first yew tree appears, and the mild Pacific allows the biscuitroot to bloom on the first day of the new year. Given the dynamic changes in climate over time, this transition spot moves, but in this century, it appears to average out right here—a temporary convergence.

Elevations < 2000 ft

Snake-Salmon System

Colorado System

Low Canyons of the West

When low canyons dissect the mountains of the West, they bring with them a variety of life zones and milder climates. Both the Colorado and the Snake rivers bring far inland a network of variety and winter refuge. That the Colorado River cuts through mostly high desert and the Snake River mostly through forest and high meadow makes a big difference with respect to wildlife. Lush summer forage, a wetter winter range, and abundant forest cover is what makes West Central Idaho a unique wildlife haven.

Inset, right: The winter wren can be heard and seen in late winter along the same stream banks as the American dipper.

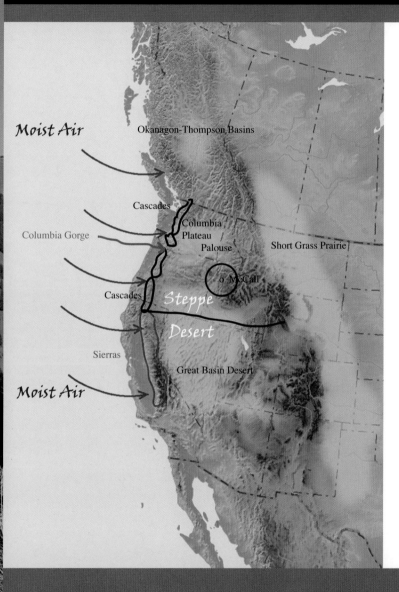

Moist Air

Okanagon-Thompson Basins

Cascades

Columbia Gorge

Columbia Plateau

Palouse

Short Grass Prairie

o McCall

Cascades

Steppe

Desert

Sierras

Great Basin Desert

Moist Air

The Rain Shadows of the West

Moist Pacific air flowing eastward is blocked by two large barriers—the Cascades and the Sierra Nevada. The Sierras are a taller and more solid barrier to moisture and thus create a more arid, true desert on the leeward side. The Cascades are a lower and more permeable barrier, but they also receive a greater inflow of Pacific moisture. All of these factors contribute to a wetter rain shadow environment here. The resulting difference produces grasslands in place of desert.

Were it not for the Rocky Mountains wringing moisture from the dry air, these steppes would run straight up against the famous prairies to the east. As it stands today, the Rockies are a network of giant sky islands, treed mountain refuges from the virtually treeless arid plains that surround them.

True desert is defined as having bare dirt between drought-resistant plants or shrubs. The steppes are wetter and more fertile, having complete grass cover between the widely scattered shrubs.

Wet Air   Dry Air

Rain

North Face — Alpine — 8400 ft — South Face

7800 ft — Sub Alpine — 7200 ft

6700 ft — Boreal — 6500 ft

5700 ft — Mixed Conifer — 4500 ft

3500 ft — Ponderosa — 3400 ft

2200 ft — Steppe Grassland

1800 ft — 1800 ft

A ridge in winter sun—a nice example of a south face aspect in grassland with a north face covered in Douglas fir and pine. Crossing a few feet to another aspect slope can be ecologically similar to a trip from Arizona to Canada.

The Life Zone chart (above) is a good place to begin thinking about the connection between ecosystems, elevation, and aspect in the complex landscape of West Central Idaho.

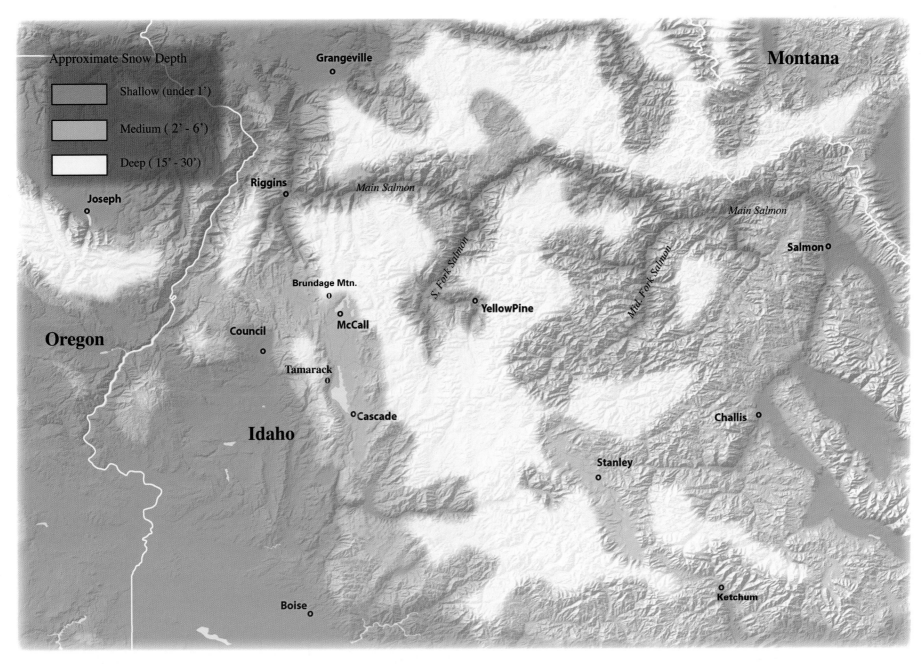

Approximate Snow Depth

Shallow (under 1')

Medium (2' - 6')

Deep (15' - 30')

Grangeville

Montana

Joseph

Riggins

Main Salmon

Main Salmon

Salmon

Brundage Mtn.

S. Fork Salmon

Mid. Fork Salmon

YellowPine

Oregon

Council

McCall

Tamarack

Idaho

Cascade

Challis

Stanley

Boise

Ketchum

Using McCall as a reference, snowfall increases in the mountains as one travels north and decreases as one travels east from McCall.

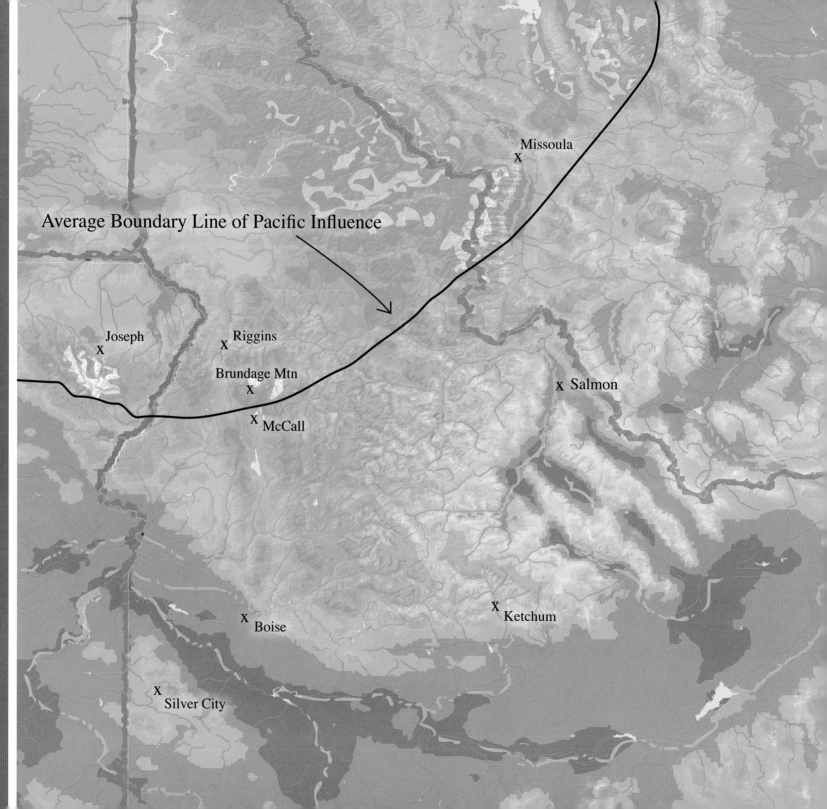

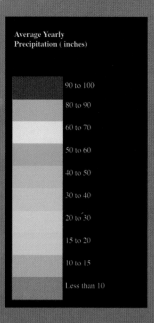

Average Yearly
Precipitation (inches)

90 to 100
80 to 90
60 to 70
50 to 60
40 to 50
30 to 40
20 to 30
15 to 20
10 to 15
Less than 10

Average Boundary Line of Pacific Influence

Missoula
X

Joseph
X

Riggins
X

Brundage Mtn
X

X
McCall

X Salmon

X
Boise

X Ketchum

X
Silver City

From this average
precipitation map,
it can be seen that
annual precipitation
increases as one
travels north, and
weakens as one
travels east from
McCall.

Map legend:
- National Forest (NF) with Developed Road Network
- Designated Wilderness (NF)
- Unofficial Wilderness (NF)

Montana

Selway Bitteroot

Gospel Hump

egon

Riggins

Hells Canyon

o Burgdorf

o Warren

Frank Church River of No Return

Salmon

Brundage Mtn.

o Yellow Pine

o McCall

Council

o Cascade

Challis

Idaho

Sawtooths

The Unofficial Wilderness

West Central Idaho is a network of remote areas. With no name, no directions, and no title, it is exactly what some believe wilderness to be.

Most of central Idaho is National Forest. With the bad economic return on the steep and inaccessible slopes, much of those forests are wilderness of one definition or another.

Above right: A Columbia ground squirrel surveys the seemingly endless wilderness that surrounds it, a stark contrast to its life mostly spent underground.

27

Pacific Low Pressure

Idaho

A series of Pacific storms signals the beginning of winter, though not everything hibernates or migrates away. Some creatures stay with us year round, and some arrive only for our winter. These wintering birds are refugees that find our winter climate milder

Winter

A complex landscape made simple by a blanket of white—the perfect time to begin an exploration of natural Idaho.

This is the view from the west face of Brundage Mountain as oncoming storms approach.

The winter storms from the Pacific keep our climate mild. In between the snows, the skies clear and the temperature drops.

It is easy for us to forget about those that can see in the dark. They live in a world beyond our comprehension and abilities. Their eyes are so adept at gathering light that even diffuse daylight entering their daytime bed causes their mirrored eyes to shine.

Right: A young cougar pauses at 2:00 a.m. near the headwaters of Hazard Creek.

White Hawk from the North

The rough-legged hawk is a consistent winter resident, seen all winter in the Long and Meadows valleys. It is another refugee from the bitter Arctic winter.

This hawk perches in the open fields north of Cascade.

Predators Cannot Tolerate Competition

When their territory is threatened, wolves will kill wolves from other packs, as lions will kill other lions. However, avoidance is the preferred method for resolving conflict. Competitive violence is not limited to the same species, and bobcats and coyotes are well aware of the constant danger from living near their larger cousins.

Full page: Pushed to low elevations by heavy snow, a bobcat rests near the South Fork of the Salmon River in late February.

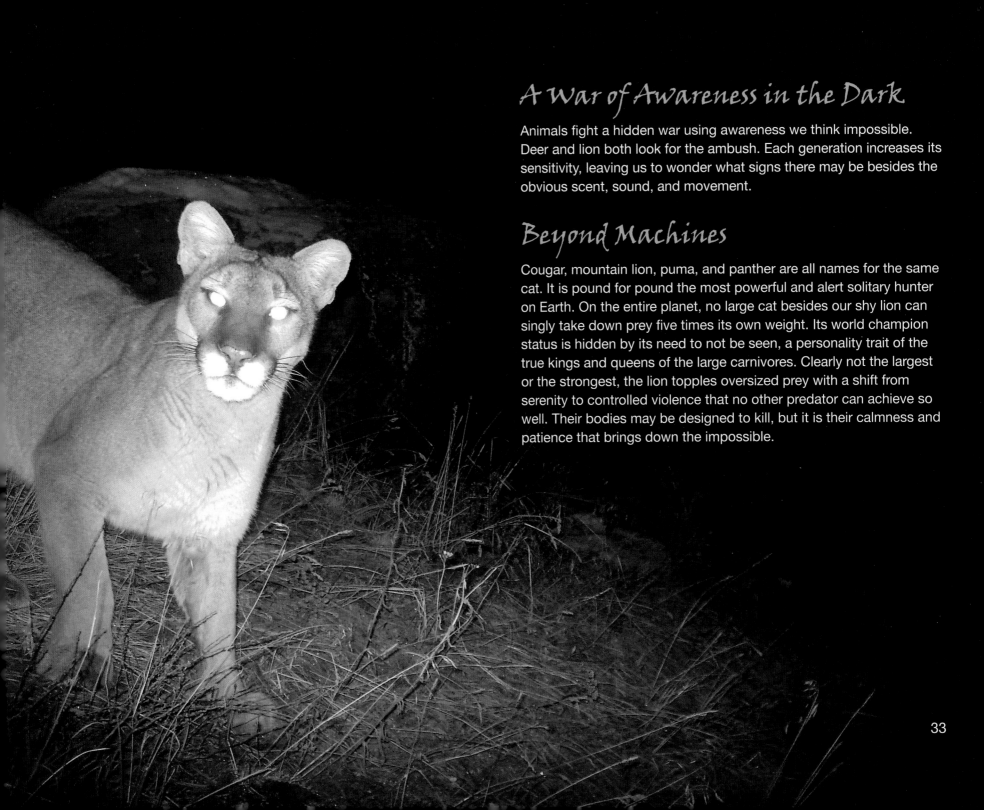

A War of Awareness in the Dark

Animals fight a hidden war using awareness we think impossible. Deer and lion both look for the ambush. Each generation increases its sensitivity, leaving us to wonder what signs there may be besides the obvious scent, sound, and movement.

Beyond Machines

Cougar, mountain lion, puma, and panther are all names for the same cat. It is pound for pound the most powerful and alert solitary hunter on Earth. On the entire planet, no large cat besides our shy lion can singly take down prey five times its own weight. Its world champion status is hidden by its need to not be seen, a personality trait of the true kings and queens of the large carnivores. Clearly not the largest or the strongest, the lion topples oversized prey with a shift from serenity to controlled violence that no other predator can achieve so well. Their bodies may be designed to kill, but it is their calmness and patience that brings down the impossible.

Balance Is a More Meaningful Term than Natural

The Ancients

When the ancient Native Americans arrived from Asia, they found a land full of impressive, massive creatures: giant ground sloths, mammoths, saber-tooth cats, maned lions, camels, horses, stag moose, short-faced bears, woolly rhinoceroses, and over one hundred species of now extinct megafauna. It was a grouping that would have made the present-day wildlife parks of East Africa look poor in comparison. Then, in a span of just one thousand years, all were gone, leaving only the smaller and wary creatures we know today. It was a strange extinction event that seems to have only affected the largest species, while the plants and smaller animals were unaffected.

There is scientific argument about the role of humans in this extinction event. Many believe the final evidence lies with the island holdouts that saw man's arrival thousands of years after the land bridge event. On islands in the Arctic and Caribbean where thousands of years passed before man arrived, the woolly mammoth and giant sloth continued to thrive, vanishing from the archeological record coincident with the first signs of man. Others wisely say the argument of blame is irrelevant, for humankind's history of out-competing other predators for their prey is well known from experience in Europe, Australia, and New Guinea. There, as in the Americas, the story was the same: mankind's sudden arrival and usual success changed the playing field forever. Whatever the cause, what is truly important is that the natural balance of North America went through an enormous change and a new balance was found.

The Moderns

We often think of the Pleistocene as a period of loss of spectacular mammals, but we forget about the loss to ancient Native Americans, whose lives and culture changed forever.

As the environment often shapes our view of the world, so too did the Native Americans undergo a shift in philosophy. With the easy, abundant, large prey no longer available, deer and plants, meager yet powerful food, became the new lifeblood. A new level of skill, awareness, and respect was required for survival. A new religion of sleek interconnectedness was forged from one of surplus and ease. This is a foreshadowing of our own current movement toward sustainability, manifested by an incorporation of high performance technologies and systems.

The shy survive.

Elk and wolves survived with and after the woolly mammoth and the saber-tooth tiger.

The ultralight fox floats atop the deep snow; giant ears pinpoint movement of prey below.

The red fox is a predator that not only tolerates us but also seeks to live close to us. It may be the only predator that walks the line between wild and domestic.

35

During a February sunrise on Rapid River, a bobcat in a thicket feeds on an abandoned bull elk carcass.

The Secret Fans of the Lions

Bobcats return day after day to abandoned kills, though they are not alone. Chickadees, magpies, golden eagles, ravens, coyotes, and mice are just a few of the other beneficiaries of the cougar's skill. Like the woodpeckers that excavate nest sites used by some forty other species, the cougar's presence has a large effect on its surroundings: the grass, the trees, riverbanks, and nearly every animal in its territory. Whether by accident or design, the cougars and wolves prevent the lingering of grazers on the fragile riverbanks, protecting water quality and keeping shaded the shallow waters.

The cougar is more than a symbol of the vanishing wilderness. It is an "umbrella" species, in that if we know we have preserved a healthy population of lions, we have a shield or umbrella that has preserved the needs of all those beneath it.

Top: Infrared photographs show a bobcat cleaning up an elk kill.

Right: A black-capped chickadee is getting its winter protein.

On the quiet ridges far from the nearest dirt roads, life passes quietly, though at rare times it can be full of excitement.

Winter Irruptives

There is a special group of birds that appears irregularly and unexpectedly outside of their normal ranges: the winter irruptives. They are sometimes very noticeable when they do arrive. The waxwing, the pine grosbeak, the crossbill, and, more rarely, the northern hawk and snowy owl comprise the main members of these irregular visitors. Visitation fluctuates with the severity of the winters to our north.

Full page: The pine grosbeak, a local but higher elevation bird, descends to our towns to eat berries and buds.

Definition of irruption: "to appear suddenly and in great numbers"

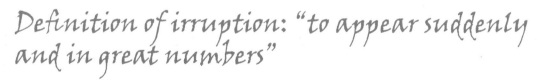

Bohemian waxwings flock in downtown McCall, a common sight during most winters.

Colorful Winter Flocks

Red, gold, orange, olive, and mixtures make these flocks a beautiful sight when they descend to a cone-laden spruce. The red crossbill lives with us year-round and will nest anytime it finds a big seed crop. During some winters, their populations increase noticeably in our towns, as birds come from farther away to join our local residents.

The red crossbill has the only bill designed to open the closed scales of the conifer cone.

Variety in the Transition Zone: Our Three Chickadees

The chestnut-backed chickadee (below left) is a bird of the Pacific Northwest coast, the Cascades, and the Idaho panhandle. It reaches its southernmost range around McCall. Its presence signals the very beginning of the Pacific influence on the Rockies. As it disappears south and east of us, so also does the influence from the Pacific Ocean fade away.

The black-capped chickadee (below center) is a little shyer than the mountain chickadee and leans toward the lower elevation forests, five thousand feet and below.

The mountain chickadee (below right) is most definitely the chickadee of the highlands. Unfazed by our daily accumulation of winter snow, it feeds during snowfall and sun, only finding it wise to hide on the rare occasions when the wind becomes strong. This one sits with its feet on its favorite insulating nest material. Its right foot rests on usnea lichen (bright green) and its left foot on horsehair lichen.

Chestnut-backed chickadee
Black-capped chickadee
Mountain chickade

Poison and Medicine

The chemicals that plants use to protect themselves from grazing are often those that protect us from the ailments that "graze upon us."

The horsehair lichen family (left), which has both edible and nonedible members, is an abundant hanging fixture in our moist forests. It uses the tree for support only and photosynthesizes its own food. Wildlife eat and make nests from the fibers, and local tribes wove this weak but abundant fiber into quick ropes and baskets.

Usnea is another of our many tree lichen species. It is one the Nez Perce used medicinally for its antibiotic qualities. Scraping the central stem reveals an elastic white cord that is the key to its identification. We have lost our taste for the bitter, but that is where the medicinal power of the plant resides.

Lichen is a partnership organism made up of a fungus and an algae in cooperation.

43

Palouse Grassland (Historic)

Riggins

The Palouse Prairie in Winter

It seems only the snowy owl (inset) would love this open, windswept terrain of the pure grassland.

The historic Palouse grassland, now cultivated, spanned from Grangeville, Idaho, to Spokane, Washington. The Palouse and the Columbia Plateau receive regular wintering visits from the snowy owl. During harsh winters in southern Canada, the birds push south to the West Central valleys and beyond, appearing in the flatlands as far south as Nevada and Utah, and even beyond.

By late January, the repetitive whistle-like hoots of the pygmy owl can be heard from the low-elevation north slope forests.

West Central Idaho hosts some of the finest wintering grounds in North America. These undeveloped and remote grasslands are fed moisture from the Pacific, while experiencing mild temperatures in the lowest elevation canyons. Low winds and reliable north slopes of dense conifers provide cover. These winter refuges contain a perfect combination of food and protective cover for the grazers and browsers.

45

Tree Islands in the Grasslands

Above: A "Canadian" owl perches in a Columbia Plateau tree island.

In a dense and endless tract of forest, such as those that frequently cover much of central and northern Idaho, it can be very difficult to locate the forest hawks and owls. There are nearly infinite roosting sites, and though populations may be more numerous here than elsewhere, they are spread out through the forest. In the steppes and grassland valleys, however, trees are a rarity and exist as little islands, an oasis of good vantage for the raptors. The Palouse Prairie, the greater shrub steppe of the Columbia Plateau, the steppes of Council, and Long Valley are all examples of open areas where an island of trees will attract a concentration of raptors. The tree island is as reliable an attractor as the water hole in a desert.

Right: A Cooper's hawk rests in a tree island in Meadows Valley.

Late Winter Courtship of the Ravens

Ravens are happy in the wilderness, but they seem happier with us, or, at the very least, more plentiful. Our living habits are very attractive to the versatile ravens. Wolves and humans attract the most intelligent of birds.

Above right: Synchronized flying begins in late winter.

Below right: Ceremonial gift-giving

As they are "gifting" each other little cones and twigs, often useless items, it becomes clear that it is the thought that counts.

47

Deer Make Grass. Elk Make Shrubs.

Deer lean toward feeding on twigs, bark, leaves, and buds; they are what we call browsers. Elk lean toward feeding on grasses; they are grazers. These rules are not strictly obeyed and vary with the seasons. The pattern is a product of millennia: browsers trim the shrubs, while grazers trim the grasses, each favoring the conditions for the other.

The local mammals and birds that stay with us either remain at high elevation and endure the snow or move downstream to the deeper protected valleys, so low that some cold-sensitive plants were able to survive even at the peak of glacial advance.

The Natural Posture of Wild Animals

An encounter with a wild animal is a thrilling, captivating moment—a rare experience with a living being that at rest and in motion exudes perfect posture. This posture is not a conscious effort, but a necessary habit for creatures that live close to danger at every moment, and use posture to read subtle signs in the infinite surroundings.

The Clark's nutcracker prefers the pines. In winter, nutcrackers flock in noisy colonies in the mild forests of ponderosa pine. In summer, their range expands to include the pines of lodgepole and whitebark in the middle and upper slopes.

The winter birds endure days of relentless snow. It is the wind, from which the forest offers protection, that is their biggest danger.

The hairy woodpecker (above left), the most widespread woodpecker in North America, is one of many that strongly affect the ecosystem through excavating nest sites and hunting down tree attacking insects. The cavities it creates benefit dozens of animals, most of which consume the insects that parasitize the plant community. The chickadee and the nuthatch are the two most common nesters in the cavities that woodpeckers leave behind.

The Steller's jay (above right) is the most often encountered and aggressive of our jays. Its noisy habit is a great contrast with the sweeter gray jay that seems to favor the higher elevations. The trend wherein jays with crests upon their heads are more aggressive than the crestless species holds true throughout North America.

On the migration to the treeless Arctic breeding grounds, sudden storms drive the swans, geese, and any other migrants down to the ground for safety. When the storm subsides, they journey on.

Right: Tundra swans rest on Payette Lake in an early March snowstorm.

As deep snow continues its accumulation on the middle to high slopes, the elk and deer move to the lower valleys for easier winter forage and greater protection from wind and cold. The wolf and cougar follow close behind. It is the only time when the far-roaming predators concentrate in one area, providing the greatest chance for an encounter with mankind. Hearing a wolf pack during a late night howl or following a clean set of lion tracks are the most likely outcomes, as watching the large predators is not an easy endeavor. In general, there is a much better chance of seeing wolves, as they are less skilled at evasion, have a relentless need to be heard, and are about a hundred times more likely to be seen than the supernaturally aware cougar.

52

A gray wolf in full winter coat prowls along the South Fork of the Salmon River.

Bird Song and the Growth Rate of Trees—a Connection Where Science Expands our Reality

Botanical experiments have shown that playing recorded bird songs increases growth rates in plants from 25 to 30 percent over those plants that were grown in controlled quiet. Recorded music also increased growth significantly over the control groups, though not as high as the bird-song recordings.

Studies have also measured changes in immuno-response (chemical and hormone changes in the cells of plants when they are being eaten or even touched). When plants are consumed by animals or attacked by insects, they release an immediate chemical response through the production of unpalatable chemicals to discourage herbivory.

Left: The red-breasted nuthatch's gentle honking is one of the most common sounds of our forests.

The Forest's Constant Battle

As humans we do not succumb to every disease that enters our bodies; in fact, we have numerous pathogens within us at all times. Our immune systems fight them constantly, and we notice them only when we start losing a battle. It is similar with the diseases that kill forests: fungi, rusts, and the insects that prey upon them are always present, and much like us, the trees are in dynamic battle with them at all times. What we do not know is whether the subtle influence of even tiny birds, singing or picking off extra insects, tips the balance of the war.

Spring

The gradual increase in the angle and duration of sunlight makes water out of snow, and that triggers the awakening of the plants and insects.

Inset images: The varied thrush (left) and mountain bluebird arrive early for the first insects on the first patches of thawed ground.

Firsts of Spring

Above left: The first native flower blooms: biscuitroot.

Before the glaciers finished their retreat, the biscuitroot in the protected lowest canyons likely did not bloom until March. As the climate has become warmer each century, certain individuals on south-facing rocks have found it mild enough to bloom all fall and winter. These early blooms depend on the severity of each winter, but no matter how cold a winter we have had in recent times, at least a few biscuitroots always bloom by New Year's Day.

Above right: The first of the summer breeders returns

The male redwing blackbirds arrive in late February. They form noisy flocks in the trees above the still-frozen wetlands. Their arrival is an early sign of the coming spring, though true warmth is still months away.

The Snow Goose Migration

A busy day along a major flyway in nearby eastern Oregon

The Otter and the Eagle

River otters are so successful at fishing, they seem to have trouble quitting, even when they are clearly too full to eat anymore. Eagles are attracted to otters, as they are well aware of the inevitable leftovers. An eagle perched above a hole in the ice is nearly always a sign of an otter hunting under the ice.

Bottom right: This was the otter's fifth fish caught in ten minutes. It ate the tail and was too full to deal with the rest. Instead, it laid the fish on the ice, an unintentional present for those that have difficulty fishing in winter.

58

The West Central Idaho spring is a reflection of the whole year, occurring on the time scale of hours, instead of months.

Warm sun, snow, rain, hail, and then sun again—this Central Idaho weather pattern can complete itself in an hour or in a week. Spring is also the best time for our plants, the time of maximum water with sufficient sunshine for growth.

Life Zone: the Steppes—the Spring Greening of the Grasslands

Grasslands may seem lonely and poor in comparison to our healthy conifer forests, but they actually support wildlife in numbers not seen in any other ecosystem. The steppes south of Council are rolling flatlands (the topography favored by antelope), while the steppes along the Snake and Salmon rivers are steep (the topography preferred by bighorn sheep).

These plains have not always been treeless. Whether you stand in grassland or forest depends on your relative point in time. As the glacial cycles of the past reached full strength, trees migrated over time down into the steppes, moving up and down the slopes in response to the wetting and drying trends that followed the growing and shrinking ice sheets. Going back further, hundreds of millions of years, subtropical forests and humid air dominated this now open landscape. Still further back, at eight hundred million years, the entire planet was frozen in a solid sheet of ice, a true ice age. The volcanic release of greenhouse gases slowly warmed the planet and broke the stranglehold of ice, allowing for the conditions that we see today—a planet teeming with life.

Plant communities of the steppes change with increasing precipitation.

Shrub Steppe

The shrub steppe (above left) is a land of shrubs with complete grass cover in between. This contrasts with a "true" desert, where bare soil exists between the widely spaced shrubs. The steppes, on the other hand, are usually composed of some combination of sagebrush, antelope brush, and rabbitbrushes, with native bunchgrasses surrounding all. This is the historical composition of these lands, but overgrazing and cultivation has altered this habitat considerably.

True Steppe

Receiving more moisture than the shrub steppe is the true steppe (above center), a pure grassland. Periodic fire, as well as moisture, tips the balance to pure grassland, as the shrubs rebound more slowly from the burns. When we think of a pure grassland, our mind often turns to great prairies. These inland northwest steppes differ in one very important aspect—the season when moisture arrives. The northwest bunchgrasses have evolved to accept moisture over the winter and spring and deal with the summer drought. The prairie grasses, in contrast, receive summer rain—moisture during the growing season.

Meadow Steppe

The wettest steppe ecosystem and the richest in variety is the meadow steppe (above right), a combination of herbaceous wildflowers, grasses, and shrubs. This is the most common steppe in West Central Idaho, a place where the Pacific adds enough new moisture to maximize variety.

The topography of the steppe is as important as the plant community that exists there. The variation in terrain from flat to steep makes a huge difference to the wildlife. The antelope has protection only on the flatlands, while the bighorn sheep, only on the steep terrain.

61

Top left: A female antelope grazes south of Indian Valley in early April.

Left: Bluebells in the meadow steppe have edible leaves that taste like oysters, earning it the alternate name, oyster plant.

Top right: An icon of the rain shadow lands of the Inland Northwest, the arrowleaf balsamroot covers open hillsides in May.

Antelope run at speeds well above sixty miles per hour, moving in tight, swerving herds, giving the impression of a flock of low-flying birds. They pull away from their predators by an excessive margin of thirty miles per hour or more, having evolved to outrun the American cheetah, which disappeared from our landscape eleven thousand years ago. Their bodies and behavior are influenced still by a predator they have never seen. The antelope's speed is a subtle reminder that the fastest animal on earth once graced our continent as well.

The American Dipper

A bird of the whitewater, the American dipper is the only songbird that swims underwater. The dipper is a reliable fixture of our fast-moving rivers, a curious gray bird that picks aquatic insects out of the water and from under stones.

Left: Miner's lettuce blooms in spring along the stream edges. Miner's lettuce is one of the tastiest edible greens we have, a vitamin-rich food source for Native Americans. It was particularly important after a long winter of roots and meat.

The Burrowing Owl

While most small owls depend on woodpeckers to create their nest sites, the burrowing owl depends on the ground squirrel. When grassland gives way to dense conifers, the great gray owl takes over. Only miles apart, each species of owl inhabits a different world: the burrowing owl in the southwest and the great gray owl in the northwest.

Right: The great gray is an owl of the northern bogs and boreal forests.

The Elk and the Magpie—An Ancient Relationship

The black-billed magpie has a cultural habit of resting and feeding on the backs of elk and deer. They often pick and feed on the stray tick, but many times they appear to be doing nothing more than warming their feet. They no longer have the mammoth, the camel, or the rhino, although they most certainly were seen perched upon them by the very first of the Americans.

The depths of our canyons are what distinguish West Central Idaho from the rest of the Rockies, perhaps more than any other factor.

Full page and top inset: Shootingstars bloom along the Snake River. The Nez Perce chewed the flowers for healing painful mouth sores.

Inset, bottom right: A member of the bleeding heart family, Dutchman's breeches blooms along the Little Salmon River in March at two thousand feet and later in June on the six-thousand-foot ridges above.

The Snake River runs freely through Hells Canyon, the deepest gorge in North America, with more than eight thousand feet of life zones. It is low and dry enough to support some of our only cacti (inset, top right).

Inset, bottom right: The descending call of the canyon wren echoes along the canyon walls during a time of flowers and high water.

Our isolated population of sage grouse—West Central survivors

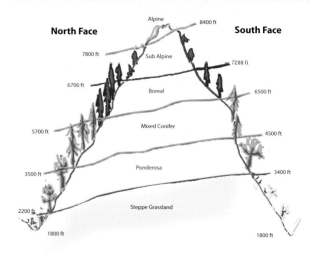

The "Lek" or Display Grounds

The spring sunrise in our western sagelands begins with the popping sound of the displaying sage grouse. Today, a few scattered groups of sage grouse still perform as the sun peaks over the West Mountain range. Here, as the sun lights the greening steppe, a group of males perform their courtship ritual in the exact same spot year after year—a location that has likely been used for centuries.

North Face   Alpine   8400 ft   **South Face**

7800 ft   Sub Alpine

7200 ft

6700 ft   Boreal   6500 ft

5700 ft   Mixed Conifer   4500 ft

3500 ft   Ponderosa   3400 ft

2200 ft   Steppe Grassland

1800 ft   1800 ft

A bighorn female stands on new March grass by the Wind River's confluence with the Main Salmon. It is a fragile population living on steep terrain. Much more plentiful in the past, their prominence is displayed in ancient Native American petroglyphs on the canyon walls.

The Mountain Shoshones or "Sheep Eaters" (in the Shoshone tradition of naming tribes after what they eat) lived for thousands of years in smaller groups among the steep slopes. This tribe subsisted on roots, berries, and bighorn sheep. The Nez Perce and Shoshone of the Snake River Plains lived in larger groups, supported by the abundance of salmon and camas fields.

69

Yarrow Blossoms

Yarrow—an Opportunity for Connection

Yarrow (above left) is an abundant plant of the open slopes, forest openings, and disturbed ground. It has many important uses, but there is one use that we may encounter over and over again: treating the sting of the wasps. Every year I have one reminder of how important plants once were to us. Each time I get stung, I quickly find and chew some yarrow leaves, swallow a little juice, and apply the mashed leaves to the sting. It neutralizes the poison, and no swelling or pain occurs. The sting site looks normal. Without the yarrow, days of swelling, pain, and itching would be the result. Once you experience this reversal, you will never feel the same way about yarrow again.

Warning: Do not chew the yarrow until you are sure of its identification. Yarrow is in the carrot family, which contains some very edible—as well as some of our most poisonous—plants, such as the water hemlock, a plant that can be fatal from merely touching a crushed leaf to your tongue. See p. 114.

A Rarely Noticed Sign of Spring

Without looking closely at the ground, it is difficult to see the Great Basin Indian potato (above right). It blooms before we ever think to look for flowers. Blooming on the cold ground of open mountain slopes, recently exposed after six months of snow cover, the bear and the ground squirrel, however, do not overlook it. Beneath its flower in the soft soil is a little potato, a tasty and nutritious bulb that was eaten raw by all the American tribes.

Spring Beauty

Spring Beauty bulb

Wild Hyacinth

Fritillary Lily

The Energy and Nutrients in Three of Our Best Wild Bulbs Goes Far Beyond Their Size

A number of Native American leaders at the turn of the twentieth century noticed something different in their horses and spoke openly about it, agreeing that their ponies were not the same anymore. When they lived out on the grasslands, the ponies drank wild water and ate wild plants. They needed little food, had more endurance, and could go longer without water. Living in corrals, they got more food and always had water, yet were half the horses they once were. One might wonder whether it is only the pony that changed, or has the same thing happened to us?

71

Wilson's Snipe

Near sunset, the cool air of our meadows fills with the sound of the snipe's courtship display. In the spring twilight you can see the silhouette of its wings against the sky, feathers vibrating an ascending whinny. As the shadow from a descending sun hits the meadows, the snipe display is joined by the chorus of Pacific tree frogs.

The activity and noise of spring is at its peak now and will slowly lose power as the season travels toward summer.

Payette Lake

The Day the Lake Returns

Wherever there are lakes throughout West Central Idaho, in April or May the ice melts and we remember the lake that was always there. The freezing and the slow thaw of the lake ice ends quickly—in a matter of hours with one windy day. The wind shatters the ice cover and pushes it into the shore and with wave action turns it back into water.

The ospreys often return before the lakes clear. They don't seem to be worried as they carry with them the memories of the Little Salmon River and the South Fork of the Salmon River, always open for fishing.

The Bears Return

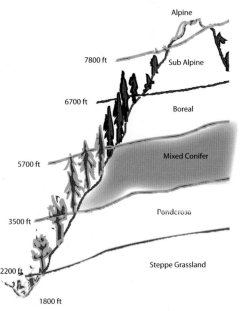

Above right: The glacier lily fields cover vast sections of the mixed conifer zone in May. Bears emerge and feast on the numerous bulbs.

Without regard to culture, humans have always felt an affinity for the bear. The Native Americans viewed the black bears as former men of knowledge, peacefully searching for plants and roots—no longer in need of the reassurance and company of the tribe.

Opposite page: Black phase black bear on Red Ridge overlooking McCall in May

Alpine

7800 ft   Sub Alpine

6700 ft   Boreal

5700 ft   Mixed Conifer

3500 ft   Ponderosa

2200 ft   Steppe Grassland

1800 ft

Bear Cubs of Spring

The cubs are born in the winter den, and they play, sleep, and nurse next to their hibernating mother. They emerge to a greening world and begin to learn about selecting and digging roots and bulbs.

The first Americans watched the bear closely, and they were convinced that the bear could smell or feel the edibility and medicinal uses of every member of the plant world.

The bear in full daylight in the open is not common for the shy black bear of the deep forest. They are well adapted to hide in the shadows and blend with the dappled light and shadows of the forest floor. This is where they feel most safe and spend the majority of their lives.

Before the first human petroglyphs, bears were marking the Aspen to announce their presence.

Right: Cinnamon phase, black bear, Bear Basin Meadow

Juniper Distribution

Rocky Mountain Juniper

Western Juniper

McCall

x

Juniper-free Zone

The Western Juniper Forest Moves in Response to Expanding and Retreating Ice

The juniper forest can be thought of as a symbol of the Great Basin Ecoregion. Inhabiting the higher slopes above the desert, it is the first drought-tolerant tree rising above the arid scrub. As the climate has become warmer and drier in the last ten millennia, the juniper has moved with it. The western juniper (see map) has been migrating slowly back toward us, into the Pacific holdouts of West Central and Northern Idaho. The movement of the juniper reflects the constantly shifting borderline between the Southwest and the Northwest, between the Great Basin and the Pacific Coastal Forest.

Plants Migrate Like Birds, But on a Much Greater Time Scale

To the southeast along the Owyhee River drainages, the Great Basin shows its first sign of changing toward a wetter Pacific habitat.

Above right: The blue-gray gnatcatcher in juniper

A Shorebird Calls from the Grasslands

The long-billed curlew may seem out of place in our dry open grasslands, and though it is a wading shorebird by winter, in summer it breeds in the arid continental grasslands. In an interesting family dynamic, the female leaves the chicks after a few weeks, and the father takes care of them until they are strong enough to fly with him to Mexico. The couple will then reunite and return the following summer to raise more young.

Two Opinions on Barbed Wire

The northern shrike loves barbed wire. It provides vantage as a perch and is also a weapon, as it often impales small prey upon the sharp barbs. The antelope, on the other hand, which spent an eternity evolving to outrun the American cheetah, now has had only decades to find a way around a head-high barrier. This animal's evolutionary tradeoff was for speed in the flatlands over the ability to jump. While it can outrun the coyote by about twenty-eight miles per hour, it must shimmy in a slow and awkward manner under the bottom wire of the fence.

Left: A meadowlark sitting on sagebrush sings in the steppes.

Native Bunchgrasses

A grassland is not fertile or productive simply because it is covered in grass. It is the type and quality of the grass that matter in sustaining life and soil fertility. Historically, the rain shadow lands of the Inland Northwest were covered in a dense carpet of perennial bunchgrasses. The deep roots held in soil for the full year, collected moisture at varying levels, and provided year-round food and nutrients to wildlife. Much of these ranges are now covered with an annual grass species, appropriately named "cheatgrass," as it cheats us of good forage and topsoil protection.

There is a balance between grass, elk, and lions: lions control elk, which preserves the high quality bunchgrasses. Healthy bunchgrass ranges increase elk numbers and vitality, which in turn is good for the lions. Lions kill lions because there is not enough elk for everyone. The bunchgrass, if not overgrazed, will not allow the growth of unpalatable plants to rise from the soil.

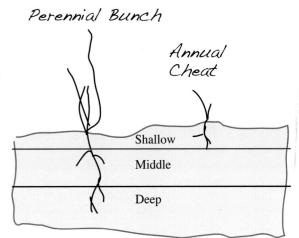

The Deep-Rooted Perennial (Bunch) and the Shallow-Rooted Annual (Cheat)

Perennial grasses pull nutrients back to living roots in fall and regrow from them the following spring. Annuals, in contrast, have roots that die each fall and regrow from seed. Their roots are shallow and are a poor soil erosion cover. They also block water from the deeper roots of other grasses and shrubs. The cheatgrass in particular goes to seed very early, limiting the time in which green shoots are available to wildlife.

Elk, cattle, and nearly all wildlife prefer the bunchgrass; it is eaten first. Overgrazing can be defined as letting loose grazers that will act to select or encourage significant growth of plants we do not want. In this case, nutrient-rich perennials are eaten down year after year, while the cheat flourishes. Eventually an entire range can consist of the low-value cheat.

Above left: Cheatgrass grows along with a few remnant clusters of bunchgrass in spring.

Above right: Bears in a prickly field of cheatgrass stalks; in this instance, gold is not gold.

Perennial Bunch

Annual Cheat

Shallow

Middle

Deep

The American white pelican arriving in Long Valley in May is a reminder that wetlands are about topography as much as they are water. The mile-high flat basin of Long Valley slows the flow of water on its inevitable path to the Pacific Ocean. Slow water translates into wetlands and lakes.

Islands of grass within the forest support the badgers, ground squirrels, and red-tailed hawks.

Our high meadows would be an empty, sad place without the chirping and activity of the Columbia ground squirrel. The squirrels are active in the otherwise quiet emptiness of the midday field. A red-tailed hawk will perch at the edge of nearly every meadow, attempting to take full advantage of a very short ground squirrel season. By mid-August the squirrel disappears for an early hibernation. At this point, only the badger still has access to them.

At left, a ground squirrel checks for danger. The ground squirrel has a large effect on ecosystem health, far beyond its obvious role as prey for predators. From its constant habit of digging tunnels and burrows, it aerates soil and plant roots. It also increases groundwater recharge and releases soil moisture to the air. Were it to meet a fate similar to the prairie dogs, the loss of millions of individuals would have the same disastrous effect on our grasslands and plains as it did in the American Southwest and the short-grass prairies.

85

The beaver alters its environment to suit itself by damming streams to create wetlands. This increases plant and animal diversity and helps with groundwater recharge.

By merely living, every plant and animal alters its environment. Most affect their surroundings in ways so subtle that we must make an effort to see it. Others, such as humans and beavers, alter with intent on a noticeable scale. Until recently, the beaver made wetlands wherever it could, while we humans were busy draining them at every turn. This pattern has now changed, as we have seen the wetland's value to the outdoor industry, and have new insights into its role in water purification and flood attenuation. It seems that we are now helping the beaver in its quest to create and restore the wetland. As intelligent as we may be, we have turned 180 degrees, while the beaver has never wavered.

Right: The great blue heron, a widespread and adaptable bird, can be found nearly everywhere across the continent.

Mountain Bluebird

Western Bluebird

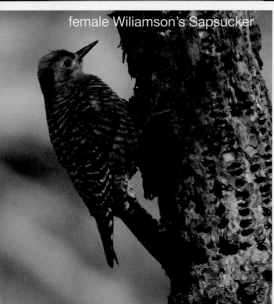

female Wiliamson's Sapsucker

male Wiliamson's Sapsucker

Mountain and Western Bluebirds

Ranges overlap in West Central and Northern Idaho where both the mountain and western bluebird species may be found. The mountain bluebird is more common in Long Valley, though areas west of New Meadows have increasing numbers of the more Pacific western bluebird. Though both bluebird species are birds of the open fields—hunting insects and nesting in abandoned woodpecker cavities—the western bluebird is more likely to be seen in open forests, particularly in the ponderosas.

Williamson's Sapsucker

The female (left) and male look like two different species, but are just an unusual example of the difference between males and females in the uniform woodpecker family, a family where the difference between male and female is usually just an extra patch of red.

87

Top left: Tree swallows

Bottom left: Cliff swallows collect mud for nest building.

Inset: Trillium—unfolding through the snow (top) and at peak bloom (bottom)

Night World

It is easy to forget about a world we cannot see. Tracks in snow and images captured by motion-triggered cameras remind us of the world that continues on, whether we are aware of its existence or not.

The short-faced bear and the saber-toothed cat could not compete with the new human arrivals from Asia, but the mountain lion and black bear, also New World native mammals, adapted with ease. A life of avoiding the saber-toothed cat and the short-faced bear was exchanged for avoiding the ancient people from Asia, as the megafauna disappeared from the American landmass.

The Range of the Common Loon

Breeding Areas

Migration routes

Migration routes

Wintering Areas

Wintering Areas

For a short time, our lakes echo with the call of the north woods.

West Central Idaho is just south of the loon's summer breeding range. Since we are located along its migration route, for about six weeks all of our large, unfrozen lakes attract traveling loons. The water body must be large for the primitive bird to take flight, as it needs a very long runway.

Morel fruiting peaks at different times, years, and elevations. It is best to watch the plants instead of the calendar. When the white flower of the trillium starts to turn pink, it is time to look for morels.

The trillium is a shady, moist, forest-loving plant. It blooms in early spring before the leaves emerge on the larch and cottonwood. It is the symbol of spring in eastern deciduous forests, covering the wet forest floors in April and May. Before the rise of the Rockies created the rain shadow prairie, forests extended unbroken from coast to coast. Our trillium has been separated for at least sixty million years from its relatives in the East.

At left (top) and above right, the morel mushroom is a much-hunted delicacy.

At left (bottom), the western trillium blooms white, then slowly turns pink after a couple of weeks, and finally magenta before going to seed.

91

The Kill as a New Beginning

Above: Wolf feeding sequence on the Bear Plateau near the bitterroot fields.

There were times when a fresh wolf kill could save lives hanging in the balance, especially those separated from their people. Winter was no guarantee for successful hunting conditions, even with maintained bows. A fresh wolf kill provided days of meat, new sinew and rawhide for bows, friction sets, and tools, and a skin for warmth and new moccasin soles. They saved lives with only their mouths, their little bodies, and the wildness inside them.

A fear of man from beginning to end: Did the now-extinct dire wolf not have the same innate desire to avoid us? Or did man and the gray wolf out-compete them to extinction?

To Die of Loneliness

It is difficult for a wolf to survive without its pack. Wolves are fragile, in need of social contact, and they have never learned to live like the cats, in silence and in hiding. They need to call out to each other, even if it brings in their enemies.

To the people who lived with them out under the open skies, they were known as the "big mouths." Lying under the stars in the lonely quiet, when a pack begins to howl, sound filling the dark void—whether the feeling is relief, love, or hate—wolves force everyone to feel.

Top right: The sight of a wolf attracts scavengers.

93

The True Complexity of Relationships

The naturalist would like to see more wolves, the hunter less, and the rancher never asked for even one.

The biologist and coyote have complicated opinions.

The salmon and the trout want enough wolves to keep grazers from lingering along the riverbanks.

The native grasses want more wolves; the cheat grasses want more grazers. Both cattle and elk want the native grasses, not the cheat.

Roots and bulbs were gathered in the fall when the plants' energy (sugar) was drawn back below ground.

In the fall, with the flowers gone, the camas and death camas look very similar. For Native Americans, it was also the best time to harvest and collect edible camas bulbs. In spring, when the two plants were seen flowering side-by-side, tribal members would go through the field and bend the stalks of the camas so they could quickly identify the correct, edible plants that fall.

Warning: Before tasting any plants, spend one full growing season learning all about the common ones—both the edible and the poisonous. Safe plant sampling comes from knowing the full range of possible poisonous look-alikes and learning all the plant families that live in the area.

Right: The vast fields of camas (shown here by Little Payette Lake in June) made it an important staple of the Nez Perce and the Shoshone.

Below: Camas and death camas (white bloom)

95

Life Zone: the Ponderosas—also the Zone of Winter Refuge for Wildlife

Inset, top right: "Candles" are the new growth of the pines in early June.

Inset, bottom right: Same shoots as above have needles in mid-July.

Pine candles

Leopard Lily

Steer's-head

Pine shoots

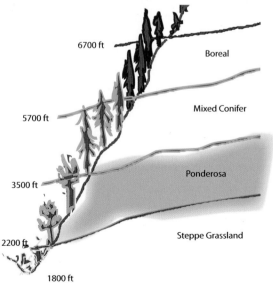

Spring in the ponderosas and the mixed conifers brings a familiar sound—the drumming sound of the ruffed grouse displaying on an old hollow log. Although a true symbol of spring, their winter behavior is just as interesting. For the winter season, the grouse grow projections off their toes, acting like winter snowshoes. They also dive into soft snow to stay warm and disappear.

Green grass in the low ponderosas and deep snow at high elevations keeps the grazers and the predators at low elevations throughout the spring.

Above right: Ruffed grouse performing wingbeat drumming display.

6700 ft

Boreal

5700 ft

Mixed Conifer

3500 ft

Ponderosa

2200 ft

Steppe Grassland

1800 ft

Columbia Ground Squirrel

Abundant throughout Inland Northwest
Large: 11" with reddish face, chest, and forelegs
Long, fluffy tail kept low
Large head and ears
Mounded dirt around burrow
Common and widespread in Idaho, Oregon, Washington

North Idaho Ground Squirrel

Only found in West Central Idaho
Small: 6" with grayish-tan face and red on snout only
Short tail held high when running
Little head and ears; big eyes
Flat burrow hole under rock or log
Extremely rare—fewer than five hundred remain and all are in West Central Idaho

Both squirrels are valuable: one is the rarest in the world, and the other is critical to the predator/prey balance, soil and plant health, and groundwater recharge.

The Ponderosa—the Pine of the West

The map at right shows the extent of the ponderosa pine in the West—four subspecies and the closely related Arizona pine. The Northern Plateau and the Pacific species are larger, with the characteristic orange-flaked, vanilla-scented bark. The variety particular to our region is the Northern Plateau ponderosa, and its distribution closely outlines the greater Inland Northwest ecoregion. As can be seen from the map, the ponderosas disappear south and east of the West Central Idaho boundary. To the south they do not reappear until southern Utah, where the conditions are mild enough for the Rocky Mountain subspecies to thrive. Traveling eastward, the ponderosa reappears, not where it becomes mild, but where summer moisture returns on the eastern foothills of the Rockies. Where the ponderosa does not grow tells us as much about the pine as those places where it does. Simplifying a great deal, we can say that this western pine is adapted to drought and cold, but given a certain combination of the two, it cannot survive.

The Pacific and Northern Plateau subspecies are nearly identical, both growing to massive size, bringing a burnt orange color to the forest and a vanilla scent to the air.

Range Map of the Four Subspecies of *Pinus ponderosa* and the closely related *Pinus arizonica*

Northern Plateau (ponderosa)

Rocky Mountain (scopulorum)

Pacific (benthamiana)

Ponderosa Absent

McCall

Southwestern (brachyptera)

Pinus Arizonica

99

Life in the Pines

The ponderosa pine forest is a low-intensity-fire forest. The mature forest is park-like with an open understory kept clear by frequent low-temperature fires.

The ponderosa is the first forest one encounters rising from the steppes, responding to the increase in moisture and elevation. It is the transition forest between the open grasslands and the dense conifers of the high slopes. It requires periodic low intensity fires for its long-term survival, as the flames eliminate the seedlings of the shade-tolerant trees, such as the Douglas fir and grand fir, trees that would otherwise slowly take over the forest, bringing darkness to the forest floor, increasing the fuel density while decreasing the variety of grasses and shrubs. The summer droughts and frequent dry lightning strikes of the Inland Northwest have kept these forests mature and open, although it is clear the Native Americans knew to help the process for the benefit of their game. We have recently returned to the practice of setting frequent low-intensity fires in place of suppression, which only leads to catastrophic ecological disasters.

In summer, healthy ponderosa stands, like the one at right, support the flammulated owl, a tiny migratory owl that hunts insects in the ponderosa zone and emits a tiny, repetitive hoot during the quiet nights of early summer.

Bottom left: Range of the White-headed Woodpecker

The white-headed woodpecker (bottom right), though not our most visible or common woodpecker, is an important indicator species for mature ponderosa forests, where it lives exclusively. It is present in Idaho only on the western side of our area, stopping just west of New Meadows.

100

West Central Idaho

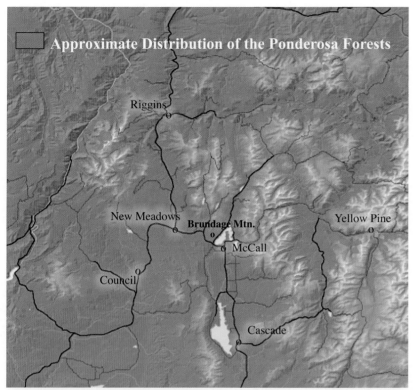

Approximate Distribution of the Ponderosa Forests

Riggins

New Meadows Brundage Mtn.

Yellow Pine

McCall

Council

Cascade

Good winter habitat for wildlife often coincides with desirable conditions for human use. The lesser snowfall and milder winters in the ponderosa zone allow for road building and easy access for development and logging, with fire suppression practices a natural consequence of property protection. For these reasons, the range of this beautiful forest is smaller now than it has been historically shown at left. Still, the ponderosa dominates the lower slopes of much of West Central Idaho and, more than any other tree, remains our symbol.

Below, left: A white-headed woodpecker quietly drills cones for seeds near Lick Creek and Bear Plateau. This bird is our quietest woodpecker.

Below, right: "Healing smoke of the tribes," the kinnikinnick grows under the pines.

101

The wood duck depends on our largest woodpecker, the pileated (above left), to excavate its nest. It is the only woodpecker that makes cavities big enough for the colorful tree-nesting duck.

Our breeding tropical birds arrive to a land of little competition, very few snakes, and an abundance of insects. The dangers of migration are far outweighed by the advantages, and our forests benefit from the assurance that the insect infestation will never go too far.

Right, bottom: Trees feed the aphids, and aphids produce food for ants. Ants also protect aphids. Warblers and chickadees eat the aphids and, in so doing, protect the trees.

Yellow-rumped warbl

Eye Contact in Predators

There is something Native Americans once taught about eye contact. It is believed that all predators, ourselves included, can feel invisible eyes upon them. An otherwise unseen creature will suddenly be visible if it mistakenly gazes at a previously unaware set of eyes. It is an awareness that predators have developed more than the grazers, which, if they cannot smell you and don't see you move, will go about their activities in oblivion. That this awareness may go much further than the five senses may forever be a matter of discussion and argument.

Intuition and Manual Override

Part luck and part persistence allowed me the perfect conditions to photograph a wolf at a fresh kill. The wind and lighting were right for absence of scent and lens glare. I was camouflaged and ready, a healthy scope-distance away. I waited during his sleep and knew he was oblivious of my presence. The wolf emerged from a nap in a thicket near its kill, yawned, and walked slowly up a rise to begin feeding again. In profile, he suddenly froze, swung his head toward me, and stared directly at me through my distant scope. His stare was unbroken for nearly ten minutes, as his inner feeling battled with his logical mind. I made no movement; there was no scent and no glare—nothing to alert him. Eventually he relaxed as he told himself the feeling inside was wrong. I was then able to watch him feed and rest, as if he were alone and safe. He continued to check all directions for any new possible danger, but he never lingered on my scope position again. Our similarity to canines is no doubt part of their appeal, and just as they do, we often discount our intuition, when it is clearly correct.

Pairing and Courtship of the Sandhill Cranes

Around the middle of spring, the valley air fills with the primitive calls of the sandhill cranes as they dance to reaffirm their commitments.

104

From the rich soil of the mature forest, the first orchid of the year, the calypso orchid, blooms. There is excitement in discovering a flower for the first time.

Visiting it each year after the long absence, an automatic smile appears. Only our first Americans and a few plant physiologists have understood that the plant "smiles" back.

Above: The fragrant and beautiful flower of the calypso orchid blooms above a bulb that Shoshone girls ate to increase their attractiveness to the opposite sex.

Caliope Summer and Winter Homes

Summer Breeding

West Central Idaho

Migration Route

Wintering

The Smallest Long-Distance Migrant in the World

When the hummingbirds come back in late May, it often feels like the first day of summer. However, cooler temperatures, rain, and snow are still likely for another month. This puts North America's smallest birds at risk, since they do not have the body mass or energy reserves to endure the cold for very long.

The calliope, as well as our other two hummingbirds, the rufous and the black-chinned, hibernate every night to conserve enough energy to survive until morning. Their heart rates slow, their body temperatures drop, and then every morning they come back to life to visit their first flower and first nectar meal of the day.

Full page: Calliope male displays its throat patch to establish its territory.

The Singing Dog

Though the coyote is often thought of as a nuisance or as too common to be worth attention, everything changes when we cannot see them, and the lonely darkness is broken by a late-night serenade from a coyote pair. Their calls emerge from them with such feeling that it moves us to wonder about them and about ourselves. The coyote touched Native American hearts as well, as they often projected their feelings onto the little dog, and referred to the "sad song of the little big mouths."

The Aspen Grove

Right: The first group of hot sunny days in mid-May causes the swollen buds of the Aspen to open.

The nuthatch (below) and the chickadee are the first birds to nest in abandoned sapsucker holes.

The Red-naped Sapsucker and the Aspen Forest

Above: Aspen trees are the first to colonize disturbed sites, such as avalanche chutes, burns, and forest clearings.

The red-naped sapsucker (inset) is a summer fixture of the aspen grove, drilling sap holes and excavating nesting cavities. Over time it fills the grove with nest sites for insectivorous birds. On the preceding page, the nuthatch is cleaning out a sapsucker cavity for its own use.

Above: Westerly view from the bitterroot fields of the Bear Plateau

Facing the towering sky island of the Wallowas, the Bear Plateau hosts the famous bitterroot flower as it makes its farthest intrusion into the land of the moist Pacific. It is a plant thought to have originated from the Great Basin, a plant that needs well-drained, gravelly soil and a summer free from wet roots. The Latin name, *rediviva*, relates to its ability to flower and come back to life upon replanting in gravel. It is so resilient to drought that it can revive and flower even after years of dry storage. The root was an important native food source but was particularly associated with Western Montana and the Blackfoot tribe of the Bitterroot Valley, where the flowers bloom a deep rose red instead of the usual white.

Right: Bitterroot at gathering stage, early spring before the flowers open

110

The map (bottom left) shows labels:
- Purple and Green Varieties
- Deep Rose Flowers
- McCall
- White and light pink Flowers
- Distribution of Bitteroot

Bitterroot is an often-missed wildflower. Its leaves appear in fall or spring and shrivel just before flowering in late May to early June. The flowers open each morning in the hot sun and close against the cold. The short-lived flowers mature to seed (above right), crumble quickly, and blow away. By early July there is no sign they were ever there.

Plants can heal from cellular damage that animals would not survive. Even when pulled from the soil, some can live for days. In the case of the bitterroot, it can live for years. Scientists understand that plants "bleed" and heal, and are chemically aware of when their parts are touched or damaged. Going one step further, the question of whether plants feel pain is not so much a question of science but of awareness.

Left: Distribution of Bitterroot

Top left: Rose color in Darby, Montana

Top middle: Light pink in Bear, Idaho

Top right: Dry bitterroot blossom in seed stage

111

Distribution of the Western Red Cedar

Flowers of the Cedar Grove

The rot-resistant trunk of the western red cedar (above left) is a natural fit for the wet coastal-type forests.

Bunchberry dogwood (above center) and wild ginger (above right) grow in a cedar grove along the Lochsa River.

The Lochsa River

The western red cedar forest marks the increasing strength of the Pacific Influence.

The range of the western red cedar and the range of the coastal forests that we associate with the Pacific Northwest are one and the same. It is the beginning of the pure Northern Rockies.

113

Angelica

Hemlock

Medicinal Angelica and Poisonous Water Hemlock: The Danger of Look-alikes

Water hemlock is the most poisonous plant in North America. Do not touch it! Even just touching its crushed leaf to your tongue can cause illness and death.

Water Hemlock

Hemlock

Angelica

Angelica—Medicine: Veins end on tips of leaf teeth.

Water Hemlock—Poison: Veins end on margins of leaf teeth.

Far left, bottom: If you were to split the root bulb, the hemlock has horizontal hollow chambers that ooze a yellow poison.

114

The Peaceful Snake: the Rubber Boa

The only boa constrictor of the Pacific Northwest is completely nonaggressive and has never been documented to bite. It relies on hiding for its defense. If you have faith in your identification ability, you can pick it up and feel it gently wrap itself around your warm arm.

Above: Spring wildflower displays vary, depending on the annual variations in snowpack depth and spring rains.

115

The Black-headed Grosbeak

Arriving in late May from Mexico, its territorial song is dominant in the early summer forests. This tropical bird is experiencing his first snow, if for only a short time, as an early June snowfall covers the greening landscape. Late snows cause more problems for the hummingbirds than the bigger tropical birds, such as the grosbeak.

Clark's Grebe

Red-Necked Grebe

Western Grebe rushing display

Wilson's Phalarope

Three grebes and a phalarope all in one valley—
their habitat fed by the slow melting snow pack
from the surrounding mountains.

117

The Western Tanager and the Sunrise Chorus

The most striking aspect of the western tanager is the flame red-orange of his head. It is not caused by a pigment produced by the bird, but rather by one gleaned from the insects it consumes. In a world of invisible connections, the tanager relies on insects to attract its mate.

At the first hint of light, around 4:00 a.m. in early July, the western tanager breaks the nighttime silence with a single call—a rolling double "chip" that leads the predawn chorus of our breeding birds. Not long after, it is joined by the robin, the grosbeak, and then by the sparrows and warblers. The chorus intensifies in league with increasing brightness and begins to fade only as the sun begins to attain some height in the sky.

Attitude and Plants

To the first peoples of the Northwest, the attitude projected toward a plant during harvest was of the greatest importance. It was not so much the chanting of a sacred song, but the sincere feeling of interest and gratitude that was projected to and felt by the plant. The belief was that the plant changed in response to the energy of the collector. Biologists have proven that plant chemistry does indeed change in response to the vibration of touch, the vibration of sound, and the vibration that living animals emit, although to our world of science the plant is still a machine, albeit a much more sensitive one than previously thought. While we do not often attribute these levels of awareness to the plant world, the opposite has been true for a much longer time in human history. Any wildflower or tree is far more interesting to us when we consider the possibility that it may feel our presence, for that is the way we are—beings that fear loneliness the most.

The Lower Ponderosa Zone

The Lewis's woodpecker is a migrating woodpecker that arrives to catch insects in mid-flight. It behaves less like a woodpecker and more like a flycatcher. It prefers the lowest of the ponderosa forests. Even a short river trip along the Salmon River usually reveals the Lewis's woodpecker in active aerial hunts for insects.

Icons of the Lower Ponderosa Zone

Poison ivy (above left) and the rattlesnake (above right) are found in the very lowest of our elevations. Both reach their upper-elevation limit in the lower ponderosa zone, at about three thousand feet. The long season of cold above this threshold elevation creates a barrier in which neither species can survive.

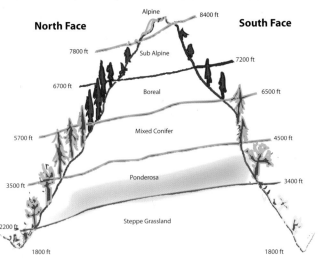

North Face
South Face

Alpine — 8400 ft

7800 ft

Sub Alpine — 7200 ft

6700 ft

Boreal — 6500 ft

5700 ft

Mixed Conifer — 4500 ft

3500 ft

Ponderosa — 3400 ft

2200 ft

Steppe Grassland

1800 ft — 1800 ft

121

Cats Have the Perfect Balance Between Sweetness and Violence

Female lions spend most of their lives with dependent young, while males spend most of their lives alone. Females have an enormous job of educating their kittens and spend almost two years with them. On average only one out of the three or four kittens makes it to adulthood. The mother shown here is down to her last one.

The Purr Changes Everything

Our mountain lions are not so different from the house cat: they spend most of their lives hiding, waiting, and resting. The toning vibration of their purr keeps them relaxed and flexible, ready for explosive movement directly from a three-hour motionless ambush.

The East Coast colonial fur traders often would ask the natives they encountered why they only saw the pelts of female lions. When was it, they inquired, that they could expect to see the "maned" skins of the males? The eastern tribes likely had confusing answers, having never seen the unrelated African lion. Their ancestors had, and the irony is that if it was maned lions the traders craved, they were actually in the right place, just eleven thousand years too late. The cougar is the purring lion, an American cat that puts all large roaring cats behind it in pound-for-pound power and ability.

Above, right: Syringa, Idaho's state flower, grows abundantly along riverbanks in West Central Idaho, shown here blooming nearby.

The bobcats that choose to follow the lions, feasting on the leftovers, always seem to look the healthiest and the most relaxed. The relaxed posture would end, of course, if discovered.

Veterinarians long ago noticed ailments in dogs that are unheard of in cats. The healing effect of the full-body vibration of all the purring animals has been well studied. It is the purr that heals and tones the body.

The Variety of the "Edge"— the Transition Zone

Most plants and animals live at the "edge." Deep in the meadow center and far into the dark forest, there will never be the variety of plant and animal life that one will find in the transition between the two. It is the ecotone, the place where habitats blend, that is the richest of all.

125

The Red Ridge above Long Valley

Inset: Blue grouse display from late May to early June in the mixed conifer zone.

A red fox hunts the ridge above McCall.

126

Fox Pups of May

The fox has learned that living close to humans can now be safer than living in the wilderness.

Yellow-breasted chat

leaf eaters

Lazuli bunting

The Riverine Forests of the Steppes

The cottonwood valleys ring with tropical-sounding calls of colorful birds.

Inset: The leaf eaters become prey and are the main reason that birds from the tropics leave their homes to come to our land of abundance to breed.

The Secretive Rails

Mixed among the spring calls of the marshes is the beautiful, almost prehistoric, call of the sora rail. The rails are secretive, shy, and disappear behind the reeds at the slightest hint of disturbance. A short and quiet wait will usually result in its reappearance and the opportunity to watch this wary but beautiful bird.

129

The Future of the Pack

Wolf dens are often located in the dense lodgepole forests of the higher elevations, similar to the one shown.

In the wolf pack, only the alpha pair breed, though all take care of raising and feeding the young. The fast-growing pups, with their healthy legs and teeth, are critical additions to a family whose lifestyle takes a serious toll on the body.

North Face

Alpine
7800 ft
Sub Alpine
6700 ft
Boreal
5700 ft
Mixed Conifer
3500 ft
Ponderosa
2200 ft
Steppe Grassland
1800 ft

Wild Turkey

Queen's Cup Lily

Life Zone: the Mixed Conifers, a Zone of Maximum Diversity

With the abundant meat of the lumbering Pleistocene giants long gone, the modern Native American was born. Skill, awareness, and respect were required from this new landscape, a land that required a sleekness of body and attitude to survive.

Mountain Lady Slipper

Rein Orchid

Striped Coral Root

Ladies' Tresses Orch.

The Forest: Old Growth or Mature?

What separates an old-growth forest from a mature forest is not the living trees, but the trees that have died: old standing snags and fallen decayed trunks. These skeletons provide homes, food, and fertile soil. The mature forest is too young yet to have these members, but it will, given a few centuries more.

Nearly every plant has a relationship with a fungus in the soil, a partnership that keeps both healthy and strong. We know very little about it, despite how important plants are to us. Massive trees are believed to be as much a result of the presence of active soil fungus as they are of factors such as rainfall. Mycelium, the fibrous vegetative part of a fungus, acts as root extensions for the plant and decomposes organic matter and pollutants in the soil. As plants clean the air and provide the base of life aboveground, mycelia do the same underground.

The Orchids

The orchid should be remembered not only by its short-lived delicate flower, but also by its fungus partner in the soil. It is the underground relationship on which its roots, leaves, and flowers depend. This fungus facilitates its germination and keeps it alive and healthy. Neither would exist without the other. Although they never see each other, they are faithful with their exchange: sugar for mineral water, mineral water for sugar.

Top right: The spiral-twisted Ladies' Tresses orchid is a late bloomer of the open forests and meadows.

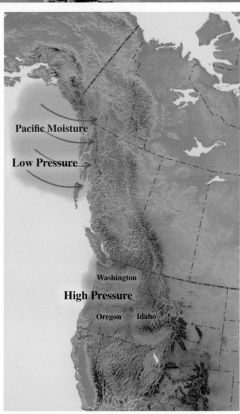

Pacific Moisture

Low Pressure

Washington

High Pressure

Oregon   Idaho

With the storm track now far to the north, a high pressure settles in over the Pacific Northwest, and a summer of clear skies takes hold. The drought-resistant conifers that blanket the region are as much a product of the summer drought as they are of the deep snow of winter.

Inset, above left: The white bog orchid is a fragrant orchid of sunny, wet meadows.

Inset, above right: Purple spikes of the Elephant's Head, a lousewort with flowers that resemble its namesake.

133

A Moose Calf Waits in Hiding for Its Mother to Return

In the Old World, animals evolved together with Man. In the New World, the arrival of Man was a sudden and catastrophic event. The shy and elusive moose was one of the many that made it through the megafaunal extinction event, having already passed the test for hundreds of thousands of years in Boreal Europe and Russia.

Inset: Yellow warblers call from the willow thickets along the watercourses.

134

The Moose and Summer Swamps

If there is one time when it is easier to see our shy moose, it is in June and July when they stand chest-deep in the slow-moving streams or ponds and plunge head-deep to grab the succulent aquatic vegetation that they love. They feel a safety in deep water, an interesting analog to their habit of spending the winter in the safety of the "predator-free" deep snow.

Moose that inhabit our area are shy, secretive animals in comparison to those that live out on the open tundra. Our moose have always had the choice of hiding amid the dense and vast forests. It is a convenient place to hide, at least for the browsers, as the twigs and buds of the forest are their main diet.

Right: The marsh marigold is found in high-elevation springs.

135

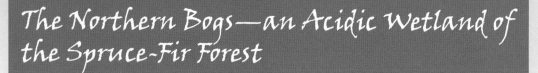

The Northern Bogs—an Acidic Wetland of the Spruce-Fir Forest

There is something engaging and profoundly calming about the gray jay (inset, top). It seems to prefer the quiet of high altitudes and in general has a completely different personality from the more aggressive Steller's jay. The gray jay whistles, soars, and seems to float and almost stall in midair before landing nearby for a closer look. Near campgrounds and homes it will become tame, but even far from any civilization, it seems to have an almost natural affection for us.

The Carnivorous Sundew

The nutrient-poor, acidic bogs give this primitive plant a competitive chance. The sticky hairs of the sundew trap insects, dissolve them, and absorb their juices.

Inset, bottom: A gnat on the sticky pad of the sundew

Reading Tracks on the Body of a Ghost, the Resident Male

The large, dominant male is the rarest and most difficult individual to encounter in the wild. There are a number of reasons why—for one, lion hunters covet him above all else. He is the "trophy rack" of all cats and, therefore, is rarely passed up in a hunt. Another reason may be a matter of his own success. The mature resident male will claim his first choice of territory, often far from people. He need not venture into new, marginal, or unknown areas in search of game or females. In so doing, he can stay hidden in known habitat, risking less exposure to the potential dangers of the civilized world.

Top: The right ear of this male is tattered, a common sign of males fighting for territory and females. Females, of course, are welcome to overlap his territory.

Bottom: The deep scar on the right flank suggests an elk's hoof or antler gouged deeply, a possibly near-fatal wound.

The Weasel in Summer Coat

The short-tailed weasel, or ermine, turns a perfect white in winter; only the black eyes and the black tip of its nose are visible against the backdrop of snow. In summer, its back turns the color of earth, and only the tender belly keeps the memory of the world of winter white.

Huckleberries

Juneberry or serviceberry

Thimbleberry

Berries

Huckleberries vary in flavor and color from berry to berry.

Left, top: The cedar waxwing is nearly exclusively a fruit eater.

Left, middle: The western tanager is a part-time fruit eater.

Left, bottom: Huckleberry picking is a good way to improve your chances of seeing a bear.

Summer is a time when sounds gradually quiet after the activity of spring. The snipe are silent now, having been replaced by the diving displays of the nighthawk, whose high-speed nosedives fill the twilight with eerie echoes.

The Most Successful Owl in the New World

The great horned owl is the owl of the Americas. It succeeds in deserts, dense forest, the plains, and any habitat we seem to alter. Their range spans North America—only in the extreme Arctic do they give way to the snowy owl completely.

The nocturnal bushy-tailed woodrat (top right) is prey for many predators, including the owl.

Right: The mariposa lilies fill the open fields in the heat of midsummer.

The edible bulbs were collected by the western tribes, as well as by the early Mormons during times of crop failure.

140

The Great Gray Owl

During daylight, the red-tailed hawks and Columbia ground squirrels occupy the mountain meadows. At sunset, the voles and the great gray owls take over. Great grays hunt after sunrise in the late summer when their chicks are getting big, and they can never seem to catch enough prey to satisfy their large offspring.

Below left: A nearly adult-size chick, able to fly but not yet hunting

Below: The abundant voles seem to be nearly every predator's favorite meal.

The Unknown Three-Way Relationship

As mentioned before, mycelium, the threadlike fungus, forms a relationship with at least 90 percent of the Earth's plants. There is a third and unknown partner in non-photosynthetic plants like the ghost plant shown above, which is a harmless companion to the fungus and that relies on it for food. This third element is like a parasite on the fungus, but while no harm seems to befall the fungus or the plant, it is not known if there is any beneficial exchange involved.

All animals, ourselves included, are bonded to the plant world. We have cultivated plants for our survival, as they have also cultivated or trained us for theirs. That flowers have trained the bees, and the fig trees have trained the apes, is as fascinating as the realization that they did it with an offer of reward, not punishment. Also of interest is our similarity with even the mycelia in the soil, as we provide water and minerals to "our plants" in exchange for food that neither of us can create alone.

The pure white ghost plant, or Indian pipe, in peak bloom (above).

The three-foot-tall pinedrops emerge from the dark forest floor, new shoot emerging (right).

Range of the Candy Stripe

McCall

Candy Stripe under the Lodgepole

Found under the dry trees of the Warren Plateau, north of McCall, the unusual and colorful candy stripe is an uncommon but strict indicator of our healthy lodgepole stands.

The Whitebark Pines—Ancient Trees of the Timberline

Disease and beetles are killing 90 percent of our whitebark pines, but it is more meaningful that the trees' natural immune systems are saving 10 percent.

Allowing the immune systems of the whitebarks to function without interference may be the only real help we can provide.

The whitebark pines inhabit only the highest (subalpine) elevations. They have the largest seeds of our local pines, which is of great importance to the nutcracker, squirrel, and bear. They are also our longest-lived trees, often living over a thousand years, although not quite as old as the Sierra Nevada's equivalent, the bristlecone pine.

Alpine

7800 ft   Sub Alpine

6700 ft   Boreal

5700 ft   Mixed Conifer

3500 ft   Ponderosa

2200 ft   Steppe Grassland

1800 ft

144

The Short Summer of the Lakes Near the Tree Line

Summit Lake at Buckhorn Pass

Inset, top: Grass of Parnassus along the slow creeks

Inset, bottom: Pink mountain heather along the lakeshores

The Deepest of Canyons

The deepest canyon in North America is Hells Canyon, where the Snake River flows as much as eight thousand feet below the ridge tops.

The pattern where our summers show a slowdown in plant and wildlife activity applies directly to the greater summer drought region of the Pacific Northwest. However, it is not the same everywhere. In contrast, the desert Southwest goes through a second noisy spring as the monsoon rains of July and August arrive.

Bighorn rams rejoin the females in the early fall, and begin the head-butting competitions later in the season. Steep slopes along the Main Salmon and Snake rivers are best for viewing the bighorn sheep.

Range of the Bighorn Sheep

McCall

Chinook Salmon Return from the Pacific Ocean

In a strange parallel, the essence of the Pacific itself weakens and ends its journey on our west-facing slopes along with the chinook salmon itself. The snow and rain from the Pacific air masses, along with the nutrients from the chinooks' bodies, are washed back to the ocean from where it all came.

Left: A chinook nears the end of spawning, midsummer, in the Upper Secesh River. White spots on the back signal that death is near.

Wolves and lions, the whole year round, keep the herds from lingering in the fragile riverine zones, preserving the vegetation that cleans and shades the rivers and streams.

Below: The water-filled stem of the thistle, scraped of its spines by a rock or knife, was eaten like celery by Native Americans. It was also used as an emergency source of fresh water during the heat of summer.

Predators and Water Quality

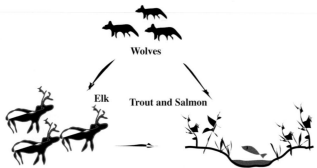

Wolves

Elk   Trout and Salmon

Subalpine Zone

In our interglacial time period, snow fields rarely last past summer.

The subalpine zone encompasses the forest of stunted trees that exist between the spruce and fir (the boreal zone) below and the alpine tundra above. It is the blurry zone that surrounds what we often call the treeline or timberline. The highest of all transition zones, it is a place where open areas of alpine meadow form a patchwork among islands of dwarfed trees. The true alpine zone, roughly defined as the matted plants and grasses that exist above all possible tree growth, is rare in the Pacific Northwest. Rock and ice often take the place of the true alpine meadows, which require better soil development than currently exists in the high ranges of the Pacific Northwest.

As the ponderosa forest is the transition community for the low timberline, the subalpine forest is the corresponding transition for the high timberline.

Right, top: Subalpine fir grows in the cracks of the glacier–scraped granite.

Yellow columbine (right, middle) and Lewis's Monkey flower (right, bottom) bloom along the springs of a late summer snow bank.

	Alpine
7800 ft	Sub Alpine
6700 ft	Boreal
5700 ft	Mixed Conifer
3500 ft	Ponderosa
2200 ft	Steppe Grassland
1800 ft	

Late Summer Fire Season— High Pressure, Drought, and Dry Lightning

Left: Fire plumes rise over the West Central mountains.

Fireweed is one of the first plants to grow back following a fire (bottom right and left). Mountain Shoshone steamed the abundant young tender shoots and ate them like asparagus. They also used the fiber from the stems to twist into cordage.

Lodgepole Pine Forest: the Catastrophic Fire Forest

The forest as shown is about as mature as the lodgepole community can reach before shade-tolerant species overtake the forest. The spruce and fir saplings grow beneath the pines. Without periodic fire, these new trees would eventually overtake the lodgepole forest. Fire eventually comes and sets the playing field back to zero. The cones of the lodgepole open in the heat, and they begin to grow on a charred landscape without competition.

Right, bottom: Grouse whortleberry, one of the most flavorful of all our wild berries, is the most common groundcover in the lodgepole forest.

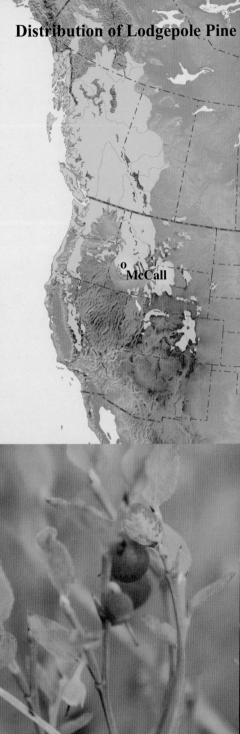

Distribution of Lodgepole Pine

o McCall

150

Secesh Summit—Recovery from Catastrophic Fire

The catastrophic fires that the lodgepole depend upon, and to some extent contribute to, also benefit the shrub and grass eaters, at least for a few decades, as the charred canopy lets light through to the emerging forage on the "new" forest floor. Before long, the thick stands of even-aged lodgepole shade out the forest floor and create fuel for the next strong fire event.

Above: Beargrass in the burns at Secesh Summit in mid-June

Inset: Aspen leaves rattle in the summer wind.

Quaking aspen is another pioneer after a disturbance. The quaking aspen trees have flattened stems that cause their leaves to flutter, or quake, in the slightest breeze. In this way the leaves move out of each other's way, allowing sunlight in continuous flashes to reach every leaf.

The Alpine Zone

This nearly barren landscape at 9,300 feet is the work of glaciers. Soil and plant cover have not had enough time to develop and recolonize.

In the Inland Northwest, treeline often transitions directly to rock, although small pockets of the true alpine tundra do exist where soil development has occurred. Two good examples are in the Seven Devils and Council Mountain ranges.

Inset, bottom: Pika thrive in the rocky, talus-covered slopes of the highest peaks.

Above: The tundra above the trees, in the Seven Devils Range

Autumn

In early September, before the leaves change, the nighttime forests suddenly begin echoing with the bugling of the bull elk. This is the day autumn begins. As if on cue, the owls begin to call again: the great horned and pygmy owls give notice that they are already thinking of winter breeding.

A bull elk bugles to establish its mating rights with the females of the herd. Challenges among competing males not solved with a bugling duel are resolved by an exhausting antler-to-antler fight.

153

Autumn arrives first in the alpine zone, a reversal of the spring sequence.

Inset: The mountain goat clings to the rough terrain of our highest peaks. It was often referred to as the "white buffalo" in the distant past.

154

Pacific Yew Distribution

Inland Extension of
Pacific Coastal Forest

Pacific Coastal
Forest

Riggins

Continental Extent of
the Yews

The Pacific Yew Forest

The Pacific yews survived the freeze of the past ice ages by clinging to the lowest valleys of western Idaho, places where both mild and moist conditions still persisted. The inner bark of this beautiful tree contains taxinol, a cancer-fighting agent, while its elastic, dense wood made some of the best bows on the North American continent.

155

The Spawning of the Kokanee Salmon

The kokanee is a species of salmon that no longer returns to the ocean. It spends its whole life landlocked between lake and pebble-lined spawning grounds. Turning a bright red just before its demise, the color is all the more beautiful because of its fleeting nature. In its death, nutrients from the kokanee's body will flow back downstream to the lakes, keeping the water itself from becoming a sterile desert.

Inset: The kokanee turn a brilliant red color before they die, much like the changing leaves that follow soon after.

The osprey, eagle, and bear all linger at these spawning grounds to get much-needed protein before winter.

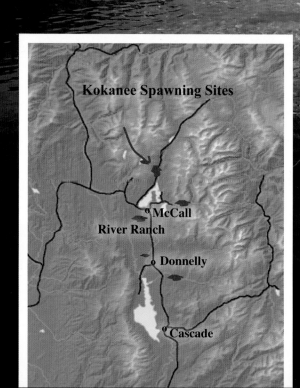

Kokanee Spawning Sites

McCall

River Ranch

Donnelly

Cascade

Yellow-headed blackbird on cattail seed head

Mule Deer Bucks Come to Town

There is a small subset of mule deer bucks that have a tradition of appearing within McCall city limits during fall. On a small scale, those bucks that like to linger near us, near our children and pets, are seldom at risk of being taken during the fall hunting season—a strange but effective adaptation. These bucks, along with the fox and the raven, are three species that defy the classic definition of wild. The photo above was taken at the corner of Mission and Deinhard streets in McCall.

A Native Supermarket in the Wetlands

The cattail offered food, medicine, and utility throughout the year to the first Americans. The spring shoots were peeled and eaten both raw and cooked, the immature male flowers were eaten like corn, and the pollen was used as flour. In fall or early spring, the roots were crushed in bowls of cold water, and the nutritious flour that settled was baked on hot rocks, forming biscuits. The gel from the stem base was used directly on bites, cuts, and sores. Its leaves were woven into baskets, shelter, and mats. The mature, downy seed was added to inner bark to produce flames from friction coals. The list of its uses continues on, but it was a crop that needed no attention and grew in abundance.

The Aspen Clone

The aspen grove is actually one large organism of genetically identical plants all connected at the roots. When a grove of trees all change color at the same time, you are most likely looking at one single organism. The bark is covered with a white powder that was once used to cover the natural shine of human skin. For western tribes in wintertime, it often made the subtle difference between hunters being seen and staying hidden, between eating and going hungry.

Aspen leaves do not suddenly turn gold; they are always gold. The chlorophyll of the growing season hides the gold pigment. Only in early October as the chlorophyll is drawn back from the leaves is the color that was always there suddenly revealed.

Upper photo: Fall along the north fork of the Payette River at River Ranch, McCall

158

Indian Paintbrush

Some flowers bloom, shrivel, and go to seed in a matter of weeks. Others, like the Indian paintbrush, can be found in bloom all summer long and into fall. The bloom at left was photographed on October 1 at about 5,200 feet. The bracts and sepals are bright red, and the actual flower is a green tube that emerges from the color. The flower is sweet and fragrant and has the same health benefits as garlic, without the odor. Eat the green tubular part of the flower only.

The Hunt

Seeing wildlife against the backdrop of fall colors may be the most difficult of all times of the year. The pressure of hunting season coupled with pre-winter access to all elevations makes for the most difficult wildlife-viewing opportunities. At left, a cow elk stands against a background of the colorful fall foliage of hunting season.

The Season

Every rural community has a joke about the game receiving the fish and game hunting calendar. The truth is the animals are merely reading the subtle changes in human activity, reading the landscape of which we are a significant part.

159

Boreal Forest

Range of the Moose

Boreal Forest

Life Zone: the Boreal Forest of Spruce and Fir (the Spruce-Moose Forest)

The boreal forest stretches around the northern latitudes. It is the largest forested ecosystem in the world and a huge generator of oxygen and absorber of carbon dioxide—a cold, often empty, forest, though it is an emptiness that we need.

The distribution of moose and the distribution of the boreal forest match closely (inset, above).

A Lake Nearing Its End

Lakes have short lives, often lasting only a few thousand years. This lake, viewed from along the Crestline Trail, was born some ten thousand years ago as the glaciers retreated, is nearing its final century. Signs of the batholithic granite exposed by erosion are still visible among the trees surrounding this soon-to-be meadow.

Below, right: The red squirrel thrives in the monotony of conifers, providing a constant backdrop of chattering sounds.

Below, left: Bull moose often can be seen in fall in McCall and Meadows Valley, learning to be safe very close to our town centers, and checking on our horses as possible mates.

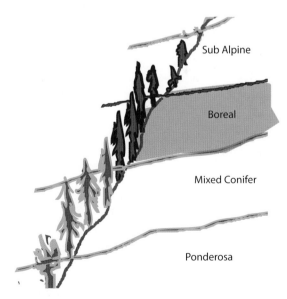

Sub Alpine

Boreal

Mixed Conifer

Ponderosa

The strength of the elk extends beyond its life.

By twisting the fibers of dried elk tendons into cordage, the very strongest of bowstrings can be made. The one limit is that it can be used only in dry weather, as water alters it temporarily back to the stretchable form found in the elk's living body.

Bottom left: Back sinew pounded to fibers and reverse-wrapped to bowstring.

Bottom right: Tendon (sinew) glued with boiled hide scrapings adds an elastic layer to the bow. This gives the bow a strength and snap that wood without such a layer would not have.

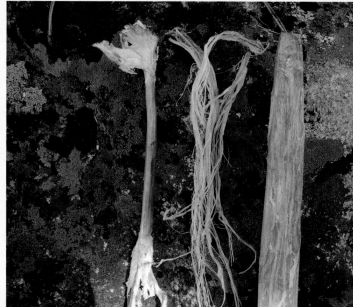

Dogbane or Indian hemp is the strongest plant fiber in North America.

There was a time when humans needed this plant a great deal. Rarely noticed, its little white flowers form a ground cover in forest openings. The outer sheath of the dogbane stem contains the strongest native plant fiber in North America. It was considered the only plant fiber strong enough to use as a bowstring, and was reserved for use during wet weather, when moisture turned bowstrings of rawhide and sinew into "wet noodles."

Cords, strings, laces, and rope once held important places in our lives.

The Western Larch

The western larch (tamarack) stands out twice a year: the gold of fall and the brilliant green of spring. It is our only deciduous conifer, as it sheds its needles every November just after the aspen turn gold. Even the evergreens shed some needles at this time, but not all at once like the larch. The evergreens slowly replace all of their needles every two or three years. It often goes unnoticed, but the display of the larch does not.

The western larch has a range that fits neatly into the ecoregion boundaries of the Inland Northwest, closely following the conditions for the Northern Plateau species of the ponderosa (maps, top and bottom). Either distribution map could be used to define the Inland Northwest as a whole.

Below: Trout moves in a shallow creek during the fall spawn.

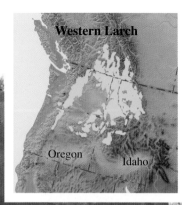

Western Larch

Oregon   Idaho

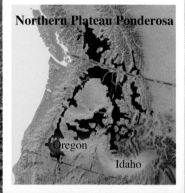

Northern Plateau Ponderosa

Oregon

Idaho

164

Pacific Low

x McCall

Rich Pacific tide pool

Anemone in tide pool

Coastal forest floor

Coastal forest

The Origin of Winter Storms: The Pacific

Inset map: The storm tracks shift back to their winter position, southward from Southeast Alaska.

Range of the Northern Flying Squirrel

The Northern Flying Squirrel

It makes one wonder what else we are missing when we first find out about the nocturnal squirrel that has lived among us for so long. Sweeter and more accepting than its aggressive daytime cousin, it appears as a dark rectangle against a bright night sky, soaring through the forest from tree to tree, tail shifting as a rudder.

If you feed the birds within the forest, the chances are good that each night in the full darkness the flying squirrels visit your feeders as well.

Above: Mule deer in boreal zone; Indian paintbrush blooming in autumn.

Right: It is less of a mystery where bats came from when we finally see the flying squirrel.

The Clark's nutcracker lives with us year-round, endlessly storing and retrieving seeds. Some birds have been documented to retrieve up to thirty-three thousand seeds in a single year. The few they "forget" become new pines after the next snow melt.

When we forget something, we're usually in trouble. When a nutcracker forgets . . . a new tree grows.

Missoula
x

Kooskia
x

Joseph
x

Riggins
x

Brundage Mtn.
x
x
x McCall

Council
x

Cascade
x

Challis
x

Stanley
x

Boise
x

Ketchum
x

Silver City
x

Elk Descend Again, the Mark of Full Winter's Arrival

As the snow accumulates with each passing week, the elk move lower and lower. At winter's peak, during the coldest storms, the elk hit the valley floors. They feel safer on the hillsides up high and travel only as low as they must to find food.

Average Snowfall Amounts

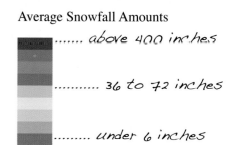

.... above 400 inches

.... 36 to 72 inches

.... under 6 inches

The Conifers

Built to hold snow, they endure the long freeze and withstand the summer drought.

Like the giant cactus, conifers store moisture in their trunks, giving the tree a high proportion of sapwood. The conifers are a forest of softwood trees, in comparison to the broadleaf, deciduous forests of the East. With ample summer moisture, the trees of the East do not need to have such a high proportion of sapwood. These hardwoods thrive in a zone where the growing season is longer and wetter. Only when conditions get tough can the conifers compete.

Everything about the conifer is an adaptation to stress: waxy resin-filled leaves that resist decay and dehydration, thick sap that oozes to smother insect attackers and discourage browsing, and narrow profiles that bear and shed large snowfall accumulations without damage.

Full page: Deep snow and long winters in the boreal zone show our ghost-tree forest of Engelmann spruce and subalpine fir.

169

The Motion-Activated Camera

We are visual animals: If we do not see it, it is often beyond us to remember it exists. The motion-activated camera records without bias or opinion; that comes later with our interpretation of the image.

Roaring vs. Purring

The anatomy of a cat's throat limits it to either purring or roaring, but not both. To understand the purring of cats, scientists study healing rates in chickens on vibrating plates that vibrate at frequencies equivalent to the purr. Repeatedly, these chickens have been shown to heal faster and have higher bone densities than the nonvibrated, control chickens. It would then seem that the purr is a healing and toning vibration that is responsible to some degree for "extra" feline abilities. The roar of the larger cats may capture the world's fantasy of power, but our purring cougar exceeds them all in awareness and ability.

Wearing the Perfect Pair of Moccasins

The mountain lion makes all the other creatures nervous; not a single one can read its intentions. On rare occasions it may allow itself to be seen, but most times it will allow no other creature to gaze upon it.

There is only one animal that drags a long tail through the snow.

Lion (Cat Family)

The closer we look, the more they differ

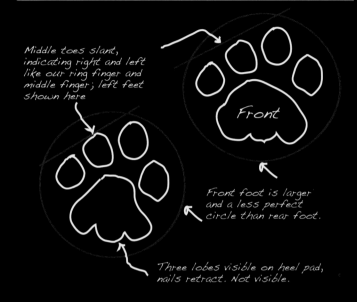

Middle toes slant, indicating right and left like our ring finger and middle finger; left feet shown here

Front

Front foot is larger and a less perfect circle than rear foot.

Three lobes visible on heel pad, nails retract. Not visible.

Wolf (Dog Family)

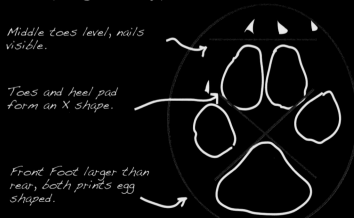

Middle toes level, nails visible.

Toes and heel pad form an X shape.

Front Foot larger than rear, both prints egg shaped.

Lions in Winter

Finding the lions

The lions concentrate their movements the most in winter. To find the cats, the requirement is not just the shallow snow that attracts elk and deer; it is also the steep, uninhabited terrain that affords them a hunting advantage as well as stalking cover. The area in orange (map) fits these conditions. In general, both wolves and elk will be in the same areas shown below, although wolves lean toward the less steep, preferring old roads and trails. The wolves are more like us, choosing paths of easy travel.

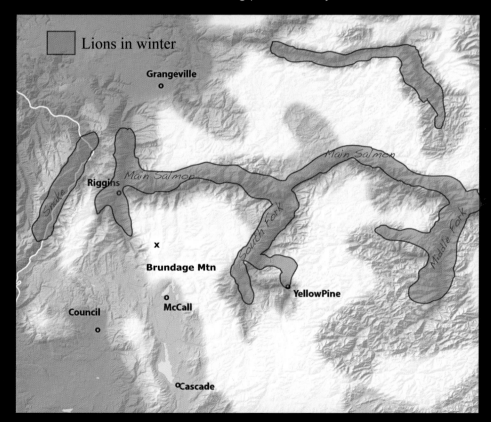

Lions in winter

173

Author Notes and Acknowledgments

A special thank you to the following people who provided tips, locations, or help in the making of this book:

Judd DeBoer, Kristen DeBoer, Mike Estrada, Denise Jantzer, Josh Meese, Isaac Babcock, Alma Hanson, Marilyn Olsen, Chris Hescock, Rob Ryan, Jon Almack, Diane Evans Mack, Robert Mortensen, Darcy Williamson, Mike Chapman, Cynthia Adams, Dennis Hart, Bruce Maury, Gabe Rodriguez, Chris Sabin, Bridget Feider, Dan Coffeen, Kevin Dammerman, Fawn Pettet, Cindy Smith, Michael Murphy-Sweet, Mike DeBoer, the team at Todd's Heating and Cooling, and the team at The Donning Company Publishers: Chad Casey, Pam Koch, and Cathleen Norman.

Edited by Cece Gadda.

To my parents, who, with the exception of my ill-executed plan to tan a goat skin in their basement, have always encouraged my obsessive interest in the natural world.

To the sponsors, Brundage Mountain Resort and River Ranch in McCall, the people who, in the worst economy in seventy years, wrote checks on the chance that this book will benefit our community, and serve as an educational resource for students, visitors, and residents for decades to come.

About the Author

Matthew Deren has a BA in Mathematics from the University of Pennsylvania and an ME in Environmental Engineering from the University of Virginia. He has worked in the environmental fields of education, research, engineering, and sustainable construction for the past fifteen years.